The Story of Robert Nabors

Sean Stewart and Robert Nabors

Second Childhood Publishing

Saint Paul ~ Minneapolis, Minnesota

Second Childhood Publishing
2541 Wimbledon Place
Woodbury, MN 55125
www.secondchildhood.org

Nabors Cut LLC
2966 White Bear Avenue
Saint Paul, MN 55109
www.naborscut.com

The Story of Robert Nabors/Sean Stewart and Robert Nabors. — 1st edition March 13, 2023
ISBN 979-8-218-40409-3

This book is dedicated to Amy, Rob J.,Devan, Amber, Blaze, Mom (Ceretta) and Dad (Bobby), Angie, Reggie and Ronnie; to Eric Coleman, and Uncle Todd Stewart

To all the BIPOC youth and adults, whether free or incarcerated; to the donors, recipients, and all the folks on dialysis, and those waiting for a kidney transplant.

INTRODUCTION

The process that led to the formulation of this book began with a conversation that Rob and I had in the driveway of his home about the potential of writing his own autobiography. He was interested in finding a way to share his unique story that not only included his background that earned him the honored title as "the best barber in Minnesota," but also his invaluable and traumatic experience going through dialysis, and being a kidney transplant recipient.

In the fall of 2018, at his family's Thanks 4 Giving event that was held at McDonough Recreation Center, Robert offered me the opportunity to co-write his autobiography entitled *The Story of Robert Nabors.* I humbly accepted, and we verbally agreed on a five year timeline.

Both Rob and I believe in speaking things into existence, and also putting the intention out in order to manifest what it is we want to accomplish in life. It's all about intention, visualization and the execution of ideas that align with our collective purpose.

We both strive to inspire and to make an impact on our community through service, teaching and mentorship. In life, there are things that you're called to do, and for Rob, his life calling spoke to him as a child, and at an early age his love for basketball, family, and cutting hair was undeniable.

Over the course of the past five years, I've conducted several hours of interviews with Robert, his close family and friends. Each interview was like a therapy session, being that Robert hadn't fully processed the entirety of his journey, and the many trials and tribulations that have brought him to this point in his life.

The Story of Robert Nabors is a documentation of a journey filled with twists and turns, a sequence of events that define him and his family's legacy, and demonstrates his faith, and perseverance that is sure to inspire all walks of life. A celebration of family, tradition, and the experiences that have shaped him. There is beauty in the struggle, and sometimes you have to struggle to arrive at your destination.

There is this term often used by folks in our community that goes *"we got it out the mud..."* which symbolizes the struggle one must go through to come up, and to reach a level of maturity and success. Let's take it a step further, and dive deeper into that analogy and how it interrelates to *The Story of Robert Nabors.*

For instance, looking at this term from a spiritual perspective, and using the spiritual concept of the lotus flower. This tropical plant begins its journey as a small black seed, supplanted in the mud at the bottom of murky waters, ponds and riverbanks. The lotus prior to reaching its full potential and blooming into a beautiful flower, begins its journey beneath the surface surrounded by pure darkness. So deep in the mud, that it cannot perceive the light, and cannot see past their own circumstances.

By design, each lotus flower (seed) before it can bloom into its full potential, spends a portion of its lifetime learning, growing and developing through their infant stages. The seeds begin to sprout, and roots begin to form, grounding themselves in the mud. By the power of the sunlight, leaves begin to grow, and help the lotus rise towards the surface of the water. Soon more leaves and flowers begin to form, and the lotus rises to the surface, and flowers open to the light. Each day, the flowers bloom, displaying an array of colors that range from purple, blue, orange, yellow and white. And when night falls, the lotus flower goes inward, sinking back into the mud and water, then remerges into its full potential again each day.

So, to say that Robert "*got it out the mud*," is an understatement, and a testament to what he's gone through to reach his full potential. The Story of Robert Nabors is a culmination of his journey that brings things full circle, and shows that every struggle we face is but a stepping stone that leads us closer to our life's purpose.

~ SEAN STEWART

CHAPTER 1

RESPECT THE WATER

My parents had an old 70's style navy blue station wagon with the wooden panels on the side. We called it the Mother Ship in honor of my Dad's favorite band Parliament, and because it was significantly larger than the average size car. In the summers, we'd go on rode trips to visit my grandparents in St. Louis. That was our main family trip. We packed up the station wagon with everything we possibly needed to avoid having to stop along the way; blankets, pillows, a basket-ball, a football and food.

My Mother would make bologna, turkey and tuna sandwiches before we left the house. She also packed egg salad, bags of Old Dutch pota-to-chips, juice, and other miscellaneous snacks to hold us over. She crammed it all inside of a large cooler, and kept it in the backseat where we could all reach it when we were hungry.

My sister Angie would ride in the backseat with the cooler on one side and my baby brother Ronnie on the other. Sometimes she complained about how cold it was sitting next to the cooler, but really she was just tired of having to sit next to a fussy infant. Nevertheless, she had plenty of space because of how large the back seats were.

My brother Reggie and I would ride in the far back cargo area of the station wagon, where we had enough space to make a pallet with pillows and blankets. There were no seat belts, just space and opportunity. It worked for us and my parents because we didn't have to worry about fighting over who would have the window seat.

Back in those days, most vehicles were made of steel and had an extremely strong exterior. Like our family, they had strong bodies that often protected what was inside and could withstand impact, rather than folding up like a soda pop-can. They were much more durable than modern cars made of fiberglass. The interior of the car was plush, with pillow-top seats, and felt like sitting on a soft sofa.

My Dad would drive the entire way to Saint Louis non-stop, only stopping if it was an emergency or if we absolutely needed to use the bathroom. Right before we left the house, he'd have us run back inside to use the bathroom. He'd say things like, "Y'all better go drain the main vein," or his favorite line, "Y'all better pee now…or forever hold your pee!"

There was only a few rest stops on the way, which were halfway to St. Louis. While we were in the car, we weren't allowed to drink much until we were close, but Angie always needed to use the bathroom. We'd stop at the rest stop, stretch our legs, and run around for a few minutes before jumping right back in.

We anticipated the moment that we'd arrive at my grandparent's house, and could barely contain our excitement. We'd drive my parents insane by asking them the same question over, and over, and over sounding like a broken record: "Are we there yet? Are we there yet? Are we there yet?"

We knew we were there when we turned into Hallwood Court, by the collection of yellow oaks that led to my grandparent's home. From a distance, we spotted their beautiful, immaculate white rambler house directly ahead at the very end of a cul-de-sac. There would be cars lined up nearly three deep in the driveway, the first being my grandfather's shiny black Lincoln. Somebody always came down the driveway, as we pulled up, whether it was Aunt Carolyn, Uncle Tony, or my grandparents.

I can remember my grandma and grandpa, and Uncle Tony all standing outside, waiting for the car to stop. Before the car could come to a halt, Angie flung the door open, and ran towards our grandparents with her arms open. Simultaneously, Reggie and I leapt from the cargo area of the station wagon, over the backseat, and all three of us nearly tackled them. They both wrapped their arms around in a warm embrace, and showered us with unconditional love. There was an exchange of energy during those intimate moments, creating memories that I would always cherish. Those are the specific experiences I hoped to create for my children, and my grandchildren. These were the moments when time stood still, and nothing felt better than being connected to family. My grandparents were like royalty to us, and we treated them as such.

My grandfather, along with several other family members worked at the Seven Up soda plant. One of my uncles was injured in an accident at a factory one day and was severely burned by a chemical reaction of chloride dioxide, receiving burns on 50% of his body. That didn't stop my grandfather from furthering his career at the company and he remained at the Seven Up plant for 40 years until his retirement.

My grandfather collected all types of memorabilia, and the house looked like a Seven Up museum. He had Seven Up clocks, hats, framed pictures, plaques, and posters and always had soda waiting for us to drink. We'd take our sodas outside and play around in the yard. The landscape was layered with lovely flowers of every color and the lawn was kept in immaculate shape.

We loved every single minute we spent there. I remember beautiful trees including yellow oaks and weeping willows. There was this enormous weeping willow with golden branches that hung towards the ground, with a beautiful white bench just beneath the base of the tree. We would sit on that bench for hours, our legs draped over the arms, listening to the wind whooshing through the branches of the weeping willow. We spent many hours bonding with each other beneath the stars of St. Louis.

We could hardly wait for nighttime to fall, as this would be the transition to my grandfather's famous annual firework display. All of us, including the neighbors of Hallwood court, and their children, anticipated the show. He played no games when it came to fireworks and wasted no time with the small joints that most people lit on the Fourth of July. He had the giant fireworks that sounded like bombs bursting and rockets being launched into the night sky.

I still have no idea how my grandfather found those types of fireworks. It was as if he was a professional. The show would last for hours, and by the time it was over, our neck muscles would be stiff and sore, and my eyes as wide as the moon. Those memories are deeply engraved in the walls of my mind, and provided the foundation on which my family infrastructure was built.

After getting settled in at my grandparent's house, Reggie, my big sister, and I saw my Uncle Tony getting ready to jump in his car to leave. We heard the sound of his keys slide across the kitchen table, and we begged him to take us with him. We tagged along whenever we could, knowing he had a swimming pool at his apartment. He tried to leave without us but we wouldn't let him. We wrapped our arms around his legs as he pulled us toward the front door. We jumped inside the car, and there was no turning back! Although we had no idea where he was going, we were always down for an adventure. Little did we know how much of an adventure the mission to Uncle Tony's house would be.

We pulled up at Uncle Tony's apartment complex, and the first thing we saw was the huge swimming pool. None of us knew how to swim but joked about jumping into the pool with our clothes on. Angie stayed inside uncle Tony's apartment, while Reggie and I went outside with our cousin and some of the neighborhood kids. We threw the football around for a while, then went into the swimming pool area.

As we entered the pool area, we passed by a man wearing red swimming trunks, who was sitting in a lawn chair and reading the newspaper.

There was a sign at the entrance that stated "No Lifeguard On Duty." We paid no mind to either the man reading the newspaper or the sign, and continued running and chasing each other, playing around the edge of the pool.

We took a break, and some of the other kids began to remove their shoes and socks, getting ready to swim. Reggie and I had never taken swimming lessons before and didn't know how to swim, and both hesitant to get in the water. But seeing the other kids jumping in, splashing and doing cannonballs, I decided to get inside of the pool. I started in the shallow end where my feet could touch and continued to tiptoe further toward the deep end. I moved along the side, holding onto the edge until my feet could no longer touch the bottom. Suddenly my hand slipped off the ledge and I started to drift away from the edge toward the middle of the pool, and further into the deep end. I flailed my arms in a panic, and before I could call for help; I started sinking like the Titanic. It felt like I had cinder blocks attached to my feet. I could see myself sinking further and further from the surface toward the bottom of the pool, then my vision got blurry.

Reggie noticed me flailing, and sinking as my body disappeared, and slowly faded away. He screamed frantically, "Somebody help! My brother is drowning!"

Angie heard Reggie screaming all the way from uncle Tony's apartment. She immediately bolted out of the door and ran desperately in the direction of Reggie's cracking voice.

My lifeless body hit the floor of the pool, and I drifted off into that gray space. It was like my body was being separated from my spirit, and I was having an out of body experience. I could only describe it as being in between worlds and I was on the verge of death. I envisioned myself at my own funeral along with my family members mourning, as they looked at my eight year old body laying in a wooden casket. My mother stood over me sobbing with the grief of losing her first born son. It was like I was standing beside her watching the whole thing.

Meanwhile, the man in the red shorts dropped his newspaper and jumped up from the reclining lawn chair. He dove into the swimming pool like a gold medal winning olympic diver. He retrieved me from the bottom of the pool, then pulled me up to the surface. "Everybody move out of the way!" he yelled at the crowd. Then he laid my limp body on the ground. He began doing CPR to pump the water out of my saturated lungs. Finally, I coughed up water and was gasping for air. I opened my eyes and realized that I was alive…I was alive!

I remember them lifting me over the fence, and carrying me back to Uncle Tony's apartment. We sat on the stoop in disbelief of what just happened. My first thought was that my parents were going to kill me! I had survived one encounter with death but surely wouldn't survive another. The car ride back to my grandparents house was utterly silent. My uncle, Reggie, Angie and I were in total shock. What were we supposed to tell my parents? Uncle Tony hugged the steering wheel the entire way with his eyes open wide, knowing he would have to face the music.

When we got back to my grandparents house, we walked through the door and explained to them what happened. My grandfather almost strangled uncle Tony, and I thought we were going to witness another death. Luckily, they spared his life. From that day forward, things would be different when we visited St. Louis, and I gained a whole new perspective on life. The family never spoke about that day again. Reggie and I were exhausted and went into the bedroom to take a nap. What if I would've died in that water? What if that man didn't decide to jump in the pool and save my life? *What if?* I had so many thoughts running through my head.

Not only would we likely never go to Uncle Tony's house again, but the fact that I nearly drowned in a hood swimming pool in Saint Louis, would impact our relationship with water moving forward. If we learned anything that day, it was to always respect the water.

CHAPTER 2

FAMILY TIES

I was born in St. Louis, Missouri in October of 1975, four days following arguably one of the greatest heavyweight boxing matches in the Thrilla In Manila. I relocated to Saint Paul, Minnesota with my mom, dad and sister when I was just a few months old. I grew up in the Rondo and Frogtown neighborhoods in the heart of Saint Paul. Originally we lived at 1008 Ashland Avenue in the early 80's, then moved to 905 Sherburne Avenue, between Avon and Victoria Street. Years later, we'd move back onto Ashland at 774.

My Mother was born in St. Louis, and is the backbone of our family. Strong, resilient and resolute, she had a competitive side that would appear in her and my Father's relationship, whether through parenting, perspective, or through sports like bowling and tennis. She was also a seamstress, and made a majority of our clothes. My Mother was the fabric of our tight knit family.

My father was born in Tupelo, Mississippi and shaped our family dynamic with his love for music, religion and physical activity. He preached discipline, as well as the word of Jehovah. He reinforced a strict adherence to rules and had high expectations for myself and his children. He also took on the tall task of having to manage each of our personalities.

Reggie was the typical little brother, the practical jokester with a great sense of humor. He is three years younger than me and my best friend. He is also a pure athlete and did gymnastics, and played basketball. Angie was the oldest, and she was stubborn and rebellious. Being that she was the oldest, she was often the protector. She would try to tag along with us but we'd leave her out of things, as she was the only girl in the family. Ronnie was the youngest brother. He was quiet and reserved, and a combination of the three of us. He was also an athlete, and played basketball.

Then there was me—*Robert.* I was quiet, disciplined and the more serious one of my siblings. The one that would tell everyone else to stop playing when we would take it too far with the jokes. I was the responsible one. I didn't know it at the time, but Angie articulated during the interviews that although I was her little brother, she always looked up to me and that I kept her going. Also, that I was my mother's right hand, and at times had to represent my Dad's role in the household.

There is a quote by Frederick Douglas that says "It is easier to build strong children than to repair broken men." My parents raised us in that regard, and instilled in each of us the values of strength, hard work, and integrity. They also raised us to be confident, and to have a sense of conviction, with the belief that each of us was placed on this planet for a purpose. Not to take anything for granted, and to never give up.

I was my father's protégé. I followed in his footsteps and emulated everything from his body language, to his mannerisms, and to the way in which he would speak. When my father spoke, people listened.

My Mom and Dad had a beautiful and harmonious relationship. It showed us a prime example of a partnership, and a sustainable foundation. They provided us a warm loving home filled with structure, self-discipline, rituals and routines that equipped us with everything we needed to function in this society.

They introduced us to sports as kids, which would become a mainstay throughout our lives. When we were kids, all that mattered to us was family, sports, riding our bikes and music.

My dad had an extensive collection of vinyl records, which we were forbidden to touch. If we did we might've lost a finger, if not a whole hand. His records were his prized possessions, and were perfectly arranged in specific order in the living room. We were permitted to listen, but only my father's hands had the pleasure to feel the texture of the record. At least we were allowed to feel the heart and soul of the music. He was a funk band enthusiast, and Parliament played nearly twenty-four-seven in our house.

As kids, one of our favorite artists was Michael Jackson, and routinely we'd dress up as The Jackson 5. For some reason it was always Angie who was allowed to be Mike, while Reggie and I were stuck in the background, often settling for the role of back up singers and back up dancers. She would use one of my Dad's old hats, and wear a sock on her hand in place of Michael Jackson's glove, and she used the kitchen broom or a spoon as the microphone. Occasionally, we would switch roles but she was our big sister, and something like a smooth criminal when it came to stealing our shine. We held a series of dance battles, and would gather in a circle, taking turns trying to turn that mother out.

The soundtrack of our childhood wasn't just influenced by our father, but also by the music that was popular at the time. KMOJ, otherwise known as "the people's station," was our favorite radio station, and is based out of North Minneapolis. KMOJ played the latest Hip-Hop, Rap and R&B, along with the soul music that my parents grew up on and loved. Because of the sketchy radio signal in Saint Paul, we'd have to use an antenna for us to hear the songs. There were times it was impossible to get a signal, and sometimes we'd have to rig the antenna with tinfoil just to listen, or all we could hear was static. If we couldn't get a signal, we'd listen to cassette tapes. I remember the first few tapes I had were Michael Jackson's *Thriller*, Eric B. and Rakim's *Don't Sweat the Technique,* and Prince's *Purple Rain.*

Prince was arguably the biggest artist outside of Michael Jackson in the mid 80's and early 90's. He was from Minneapolis, and after the cult classic Purple Rain album and movie was released, he had reached celebrity status. Prior to his superstardom, he and his band lived down the street in a gray duplex on Sherburne Avenue, and could be heard practicing from our house. Angie was the biggest Prince fan I knew. We'd ride our bikes down the block, and stop and listen.

We'd ride our bikes from sunrise to sundown if we could. And if we weren't riding our bikes, we challenged each other to foot races, always looking for a chance to channel our competitive spirit. The sibling rivalry was real, and Reggie and I routinely took turns roasting one another with jokes or roasting each other on the basketball court. Our sibling rivalry was as strong as our sibling bond. We loved each other to death!

As a family, we took trips to the closest recreation center near our house, which was West Minnehaha. My Mom and Dad would take their tennis rackets with, and while they played tennis, Reggie and I would hit the basketball court. Angie took Ronnie to the park playground. Our hands touched a lot of tennis rackets, and our feet touched a lot of blacktop basketball courts.

West Minnehaha Recreation Center had an indoor gym and outdoor court, and offered youth basketball for kids in the Frogtown neighborhood. Reggie and I had to beg my Dad to sign us up, which took some convincing due to our religion. It helped that my Dad was an NBA fan, and would run games during open gym with some of my uncles and a handful of his friends. We all shared a mutual love for the game, which was another thing we held in common.

Within the game of basketball lived many lessons that could be applied to life. However, our religious beliefs acted as a barrier between us playing organized sports, and prevented us from participating in a number of other organized activities.

Growing up in a Jehovah's Witness family was a stage of our childhood that wasn't easy, yet it introduced us to the creator and gave us the tools necessary to build a foundation with God. The religion was rigid and strict, but provided us a vehicle that we could use to build a relationship with the higher power. Our lives were structured in a way that restricted our access to certain activities. Because we were Jehovah's Witnesses, we were unable to celebrate a majority of holidays, birthdays, or join organizations such as sports teams.

This was devastating as a child in many ways. For example, when we attended school, we were unable to stand for the Pledge of Allegiance. Although, in modern times it would be more acceptable considered an act of protest and civil disobedience. During Halloween celebrations, we weren't permitted to put on costumes, and could not give, or receive candy like the rest of our classmates. We were ostracized from the class. During the Christmas parties, instead of joining the festivities that were taking place inside the classroom, we had to remain in the hallway, isolated from our peers.

When Valentine's Day came around, it was this big ordeal, when all the other kids brought in their handwritten cards for classmates. The entire class would spend days leading up to the actual day of the celebration doing arts and crafts, and making their custom Valentine's Day boxes. I just sat at my desk unable to participate. I just sulked, and stared at the rest of my smiling classmates as they gave out hand written letters, cards and candy hearts out to their childhood crushes. I was completely salty!

Aside from my friends and family who attended Kingdom Hall, nobody understood the magnitude and the residual effects this had on us as children. It took its toll on us, and at times added a tension to my interactions with teachers and peers. For years this was a recurring theme, but at the very least, I had my family, my brothers and my sister. I also had the utmost faith in God's plan.

As a family, we religiously attended Kingdom Hall, and went to church three days a week, Tuesday, Thursday, and Sunday. There, my Father served as ministerial servant, which meant he took on various tasks, and responsibilities; these included filling in as preacher, training members, doing home visits to Kingdom Hall members, missionary work, and door knocking. Also, he would lead church service all the time.

My siblings, and I were put under my Father's wing, and we participated in several training exercises and mission work that required hard work, dedication, discipline, and conviction. We'd attend church during the week, then go door knocking with my Dad each and every Saturday. Whether rain, snow or shine, we would be suited up with ironed slacks and ties, polished shoes, and briefcases. We'd get our map and move as a group through the neighborhood.

Our house was what we referred to as the kick it spot, and after church the neighborhood kids would end up coming over to hang out. My Dad not only led church service, but provided a service to many of the church members, their children, and our family and friends. In addition to being a preacher, he was a philosopher, a teacher, and a barber.

He had a second hand clipper collection, and over the years added various items to his collection. He was the original barber of the house, and started off with cutting his own hair. He would take us to the barber school or barbershop to get haircuts but wasn't satisfied with how it looked. That transitioned into him using me and my brothers as his experimental test dummies, and eventually he would cut a few friends, and family members as well. This served a dual purpose in both my Father's life and our lives. One, it provided us with an opportunity to talk to each other about life, and to exchange energy and information with one another. Two, it allowed my Dad, siblings and me a moment to be present, to slow down, and escape from the excessive noise and ills of society.

Barbershops had a special place in African American culture, with a history that stretched back generations. The origins of Black barber shops can be traced back to the early 19th century, when slavery was legal and African Americans were not allowed to work in most professions. Barber shops provided a rare opportunity for black men to establish their own businesses and serve the needs of the community. Barbers weren't just responsible for cutting hair; they also provided safety, medical care, and consultation. Barbershops were often utilized as safe houses along the Underground Railroad. For example, in downtown Saint Paul during the early 1850's, there were two barbers who owned a barbershop that housed, supported and protected people who had escaped slavery, offering them guidance.

My Dad was our family barber, and if he needed to talk to you about something, it would happen in the chair. The chair was a sacred space, and we treated it as such. When you sat in the chair, you were safe, you were protected.

He'd cut our hair mostly in the bathroom and in the basement. He used an old wooden chair from the kitchen. I can still hear the sound of that old creaky wooden chair; every time you'd move, the chair seemed to talk.

My Dad used an old towel as a makeshift cape. He would wrap it around our neck, and over our shoulders, fastened together with a safety-pin. This kept most of the hair from falling onto our clothes, catching instead with the cape, or letting it fall to the floor. I know it drove my mother crazy to have four boys in her bathroom getting haircuts, clowning around, and leaving mountains of hair on the floor. Somehow, she must have intuitively known that it was more than a haircut, that it was about pride, passion and purpose.

We would take turns getting cut, and typically my Dad started with Ronnie, followed by Reggie, then finally myself. One of the interesting things from a barber's perspective is that each of us had a slightly different texture to our hair. Ronnie's hair was coily, Reggie's hair was coily and curly, while mine was more coarse.

When it was my turn to get cut, Reggie would do everything in his power to distract me, trying anything humanly possible to make me laugh. He'd make funny faces, do handstands, do the moonwalk; anything to make me laugh—anything to get me laughing—and it worked. Looking back, I'm sure we drove my dad off the wall.

Hairstyles in the late 80's and early 90's began to evolve, going from the natural afro to the jerry-curl, to the shag, to the caesar, etc. With the influence of Hip-Hop culture, and specifically the emergence of artists like Big Daddy Kane, Bobby Brown, and Eric B. and Rakim; everyone and their momma wanted the newest hairstyle at the time, which was the high-top fade, and the Gumby.

I was no older than 11 years old at the time. One day, after waiting patiently for my turn to get my haircut, I felt the need to voice my displeasure with getting the same haircut over and over. I told my Dad that I wanted something different this time—not because his haircuts were bad, but because I wanted the new style. I wanted that high-top fade; I wanted that Gumby. I wanted to look like Eric B. and Rakim "Paid In Full."

At that point he was aggravated, and honestly, I could tell that I really hurt my dad's feelings. He paused for a second, turned the clippers off, and took a couple steps back. He asked me, "Do you like the way I cut your hair?" I could feel the tension in the air. There was an uncomfortable silence, and after a few seconds, I boldly said, "No…" His facial expression looked shocked! Then he said to me, "If you don't like the way I cut your hair, then do it yourself!" Then he left the kitchen, and walked out the house. The rest was history in the making.

CHAPTER 3

BALL IS LIFE

Before I became a barber, and learned to cut hair, my first love was the game of basketball. It was more than just a crush, and was like meeting a girl for the first time; she was beautiful, she was honest, and she was complex. I was introduced to the game by my Dad, and the moment I picked up the rock, there was a transfer of energy, as if the spirit of the game entered my body. The seams of the ball seemed to fit to my fingertips, like we were meant to be together. Let's just say that she had me at hello.

Growing up, we learned from watching my Dad and uncles play which they called soaking up the game from the OG's. Watching them play, and waiting for our turn to step on the basketball court, we learned the fundamentals of the game. It was like watching a film session, and we took mental notes, then applied it when we had a chance to step on the court. Once again, we were put under my Father's wing, and went through rigorous training exercises, and practiced whenever we could. Reggie and I shared my Dad's competitive spirit, and seeing the dog in us, he knew how to pull it out.

By the age of 10 the fundamentals of the game were instilled in us. On specific days we did specific drills that focused on certain skills. For example, we did dribbling drills in the basement, and worked on our left and right hand. My Dad used to put this orange stool in the middle of the floor to act as the defender. The task was for us to dribble straight toward the defender, and get as close as possible, then hit them with the spin-move. We'd go to the right side, to left side, switching from the right hand, to the left hand.

The person that I'd mimic would be Kenny Anderson. He played college basketball at Georgia Tech, was an All-American, and spent 14 years in the NBA. He played point guard for the New Jersey Nets (now the Brooklyn Nets), not to mention, he's a lefty like me. Kenny Anderson was an NYC street ball legend, a master of fundamentals, and had a mean spin-move with the basketball. He was most recently in a documentary entitled *NYC Point Gods*.

I'd pretend I was in the NBA, and dribble hard and quickly to the stool, plant my foot, and spin. The purpose of the drill was to anticipate and manipulate the defense. The defender's job was to hold you down, and when they see you coming directly at them, they don't know how to react. Typically, they'd make a mistake and reach for the ball. Once you get closer to the defender and spin, the defender is on your hip. Now that you have established position, and have the person on the side of you, the defender is in reaction mode. Once you have them on your hip, that's an easy layup. As a ball handler, when I have position, now I can keep you on my hip, and move you where I want to. I'm in control. Now I'm going to the basket, and able to finish with my left or right hand. There was a bunch of tactical things he taught me to make the game easier.

My Dad put a rigged basketball hoop up in the basement using an old rusty rim, and a piece of plywood to serve as the backboard. The hoop was attached to a couple of two-by-fours. Reggie and I played on that joint for hours, and nearly broke it several times a day. That was our home gym. No days off! Countless battles ensued, and while some stayed on the court, some boiled over into fist fights. That's when my Dad would have to line us up and get us back in line, if you know what I mean.

My favorite outdoor court when we were kids was definitely West Mini. We'd run and play, day and night. One night, we brought with us a bunch of construction lights, and set them up, around the court. We ran the power from the building, turned on the lights and literally played all night.

We just loved to play ball. Another outdoor court we loved to play on was on the outskirts of Saint Paul, up Rice Street off County Road B. It was a newly paved, full size basketball court with glass backboards, where we'd run fives.

We had family and friends in Kansas City, and there was a court we'd go to every time we visited. We'd run games of threes, fours and fives, all of which were played on one rim, half court. Those were some of the most competitive runs against men and women, some who played Division 1 basketball. Games ran all day and after dark, Reggie and I would go play under the lights.

In Saint Paul, my favorite indoor court to play on was Linwood Rec Center on Victoria and Saint Clair. In the early 90's, Linwood built a brand new building with a brand new basketball court. The gym had large rectangular glass backboards with the breakaway rims. Not long after they reopened their doors, they held a legendary 3 on 3 tournament, where me, my brothers and my Dad all played together. We were running folks off the court.

Basketball was similar to driving a car. I had to be aware of my surroundings, look over my left shoulder, my right shoulder. I had to look in the rear view mirrors. I had to pay attention to traffic. I had to communicate, and learn the signals. I had to learn when to accelerate and when to brake. I had to learn how to control my speed. I had to be able to recognize the red lights, and when I had the green light, and know when to slow down. I needed to be able to play on both sides of the ball.

As teenagers, everybody played at teen night at the midway YMCA on University Avenue and Night Moves at Saint Paul Central. I also played in Minneapolis for Walter "Q-Bear" Banks in the Boys In The Hood league, and won offensive player of the year. We also played in nearly every 3 on 3 tournament possible—Hoop It Up, and Gus Macker to name a few.

The Gus Macker is a nationwide 3 on 3 Basketball tournament, which had several basketball courts set up in parking lots, or closed off public streets. The Gus Macker was held during mid August either at Harriet Island, or downtown Saint Paul, outside of Galtier Plaza.

My Dad eventually allowed me to play in the Gus Macker; our team was me, and my friends Terry (Boo) Harris, Tommy Reynolds, and Shawn Benton. So we had two football players in Tommy and Shawn, and two guards in Terry and I. Tommy was already playing organized basketball, and I was just freelancing, and playing pick up at every gym that I could during the week. We got together and called ourselves the "Bomb

Squad." We used to spend the night at Terry's house the night before each game of the Gus. We'd be at his house, and get our uniforms together, then go play the following day.

There was this one year we played in the tournament, and Tommy and Shawn had football practice. Tommy and Shawn were already star athletes; Tommy at Johnson High School and Shawn at Cretin Durham Hall. They both said they needed to be at practice and wouldn't be able to play in the first game of the tournament. We argued back and forth about whether they would choose football practice, or to play in the game.

I remember telling them that they already had their spot on the team and the coach would let them play. Shawn argued telling me they had to go to practice.

Without them, we'd be forced to play 2 on 3, or forfeit the game. We stayed up all night plotting and planning what we were going to do. Terry and I decided that we would kidnap either Tommy or Shawn, and have my Dad drive the van. We couldn't kidnap Tommy because he was too big and strong, and we might get hurt. So we decided it had to be Shawn. The plan was to wait for him at Cretin, and snatch him while he was walking to practice, throw him in the van and pull off.

The next morning, we got up early, drove up to Cretin, and sat in the parking lot. We saw cars pulling up, players walking, and finally we see Shawn. We drove up next to him, then Terry and I jumped out and grabbed him! We threw him in the van, closed the door, then my Dad sped off.

Shawn nearly started crying and said, "I can't! Mr. Nabors please! They already saw me! They know I'm here."

Terry and I said "You coming to play! We got a game at 9am and you playin!"

It got to the point where he was breaking down, so we turned around, and dropped him back off. Terry and I ended up having to play 2 on 3. We played two games on Saturday without them, but lost both by only two points. Shawn and Tommy played in each of our games on Sunday, and we ended the tournament by winning the toilet bowl bracket, and earned the sportsmanship award.

The following year, we beat Sam Jacobson, who won Mr. Basketball. Then we advanced to the championship and lost to Washburn, who had a tall light-skinned dude named Moose, and (Aaron) Boone. This was during high school, all before I played for Highland Park. I grew up playing against all of them: Arvesta Kelly, Sly, Bad Baby, Khalid El Amin, Chris Rainey, and many more.

Everybody was coming to the Gus to see the high school players. Even though I wasn't playing high school ball because I was a Jehovah Witness, I knew I was better than some of those dudes. I was still one of the top guards out there, but I didn't have much recognition. Everybody else had established a name for themselves already because they were playing high school ball. People were like "who is this dude!" The players knew who I was from playing in Minneapolis, but the public didn't. The climate of Minnesota basketball was on fire.

It wasn't until my senior year that my Dad allowed me to play organized basketball, and I finally had my opportunity to play high school ball for Highland Park. I wasn't new to the game, but being that I was new to the system, Coach Portis had his favorites. Although, he had tried to recruit me to play for him since 8th grade, I hadn't earned his trust yet. I was just as talented, and could dog walk the guards who played on the team. I tried to be patient and just wait my turn, but I was getting frustrated. Coach had his starters, and I had to ride the pine and watch them play.

Half way through the season, I went to a house party with a bunch of friends. As we were leaving, I ran into one of my friends named

Londwea who was a barber. We started talking about our love for barbering, his intricate designs and how dope they were, and that I wanted him to teach me. While we were all sitting there conversing, somebody ran up in the party, shot and killed him right in front of us.

Everybody scattered, and ran for cover. The police were already outside, and were planning to raid the party anyway. While we were trying to leave, the police swarmed us, and we all got arrested. I remember the police took everybody who was at the party down to the police station on big metro transit city buses. The crazy part of the situation is that Londwea's brother has three children with my sister Angie.

I had no clue how the school found out I was at the party but they did and I was suspended me for the rest of the season. I guess because you weren't supposed to be at house parties. Everybody went to house parties, and no one had never been punished. I'm *not* stupid. The administration decided to reinstate me after my parents went up to the school, and advocated for me but I had already missed about 6 games. My Dad came to practices and helped out as an assistant to Coach Portis. One of the games I missed was a rival game between Highland and Central, and Central was one of the top teams in the conference next to Cretin. So, while I got to come back to the team, I still had to sit out. One of the games I had circled and highlighted on the calendar was our second game against Central at Central. I knew that court from playing night moves. Once again I sat on the bench, and watched with my hands cupped under my chin and I was salty.

The playoffs came around, and I was finally able to play. We played at Central, which turned out to be one of the best games of my high school career. I believe it was the regional state tournament, and we played Hastings who were ranked #2 in the state. That was by far my best game of the season. We advanced to the semi-finals at Roy Wilkins auditorium, and ended up losing to Cretin Derham Hall. That's when I was in the centerfold article in the Pioneer Press newspaper, and a picture of me being guarded by (Jeff) Rosga and former Minnesota Viking Matt Birk. I remember Clem Haskins, who was the head coach of the U of M at the time, was in the crowd watching, who really came to see Sam Jacobson.

Coach Portis never really let me play the game. He showed favoritism toward the players who grew up in his system. I understood the politics and was on the outside looking in. My hoop dreams had come to an end, but they say that when one door closes, another opens.

CHAPTER 4

THE BASEMENT

My dad was the family barber for over a decade, and dedicated years to developing his craft. His attention to detail went beyond the barber chair, and extended to other areas of his life. To clarify, my father was not a professional or licensed barber but was passionate about the profession. As I mentioned earlier, my dad had an extensive second-hand clipper collection. His collection ranged from antique, vintage, non-electric hair clippers to a set of the first electric hair clippers ever made. Out of nowhere, he would come home with random sets of broken clippers, take them apart, repair and rebuild them. He cleaned and oiled them, making them work and function like new.

My father was many things, he was my protector, my provider, and my first teacher. Whatever he did in life, I was right behind him, following in his footsteps. I was his protégé. The actual definition of the word, according to the dictionary is "one who is protected or trained or whose career is furthered by a person of experience or influence."

So at 11 years old, when he told me if I didn't like the way he cut my hair, then do it myself; I had actually been studying him the entire time. I took mental notes and observed the way he held the clippers, his hand motions, and his technique. I watched him give hundreds of haircuts. Because my siblings and I all had different textures of hair, I understood that each person had a specific hair pattern.

My Aunt Regina bought my first set of professional-grade electric clippers. Armed with the tools that my dad provided, I began my journey of becoming a barber, following in a rich tradition of generations of Black barbers and carrying on that tradition while putting my own personal touch on it. I understood at 11 years old that I had to pay my dues. I had to put in the work. I had to be a student of the game. I had to be willing to learn. Just like my Father, I began cutting my own hair.

My dad had many side hustles, one of which was a newspaper route for the Pioneer Press. He, along with my mom, took my siblings and me along with them, and we delivered newspapers to the Rondo, Frogtown, and Summit-University neighborhoods. It wasn't easy to wake up at the crack of dawn, but we all squeezed ourselves inside the same old navy blue station wagon and drove downtown Saint Paul to pick up the stacks of newspapers. I still don't know how we managed to fit inside the car with all those papers.

We tossed newspapers onto stoops and boulevards for hours before the sun came up. Our favorite part of the early morning paper route was stopping at Super America to grab apple fritters and orange juice for breakfast. We ate them in the car and ended the route on Ashland Avenue, where we lived. We got home just in time to get ready for school.

My father held onto that newspaper route for years, even after a near fatal accident that nearly derailed our family forever. My mother had some friends and family over the night before, and stayed up a little later than normal. The following morning, my dad convinced my mom not to go and we all decided to stay home except for my him. That day, while he was delivering newspapers and driving along his typical route, he heard the sound of horns blaring, and collided with a train. The train pushed him over a hundred feet — nearly half of a football field—and crushed him and the car.

My dad was not wearing a seatbelt, and they said that only the newspapers saved his life by buffering the impact when he was thrown back. When the paramedics and the fire department arrived on the scene, they found him lying in the far back, cargo area of the station wagon in the exact spot where Reggie and I would ride.

Coincidentally, the story of the accident was published the following day in the Pioneer Press, in the same newspaper that my father delivered every morning. He experienced significant PTSD following the accident, and after he recovered, he found a new form of transportation and resumed the paper route.

However, he ended up stepping down as ministerial servant at Kingdom Hall, and our family dynamic began to shift. There was friction and distance between him and my mom, and they were no longer the dynamic duo they once were. They stopped spending time together and my Dad was gone from home more often.

By this time we had moved to 774 Ashland Avenue, and I had taken over as the family barber. I had acquired all the necessary tools I needed, from learning to cut my own hair to barber equipment, including all my dad's clippers and shears. My dad had collected every barber item that you could possibly think of and recently had come home with a used barber chair. The chair had a few minor bumps and bruises, but nothing a little duck tape couldn't fix. I had no idea just how much barber equipment he had accumulated over the years until one day he said, "Let me show you something."

We walked downstairs to the basement. He had rearranged the entire set up and decided to build a barbershop in our basement and handed me what felt like the keys to the city. I had inherited it all. He even gave me a brand new cape, and I no longer needed to use an old towel when I cut hair. I was entering a new phase of my life as a barber. It had me feeling like a superhero—like Clark Kent entering the phone booth, and transforming into Superman. My family and my city needed saving. It was my time!

The torch was being passed, and I was picking up where my father left off, my hand open and ready to receive the baton. I had started my first leg of the race, but it was far from my final destination.

When I first started cutting, I just wanted to be good at it. After a few years of developing, and refining my skills, I gradually started cutting some of my family members. I was in my infant stage of building my clientele. Eventually that led to me cutting people outside of my family. Word started to spread like wildfire! One person would tell another person and another.

I think the hardest part of giving a haircut wasn't the style, the blend, the fade, the design or even the lineup. It was the ability to multitask and maintain the quality of the haircut, while maintaining the quality of the conversation. That was part of providing a service that took years of practice. My dad always used the chair as an opportunity to talk to you about something important, to share his wisdom, and to give you some game. That's what a good barber does, and what the barbershop has provided for people for generations. When people sat in that chair, it was like an exchange of energy.

By the time I was 16 years old, I had built my clientele and had the entire city buzzing. People were taking the city bus and traveling across the city to the basement for a haircut. The line stretched up the basement stairs and wrapped around the side of the house. I was making money! Everybody and their momma wanted to know, who Robert Nabors was.

CHAPTER 5

REVOLVING CHAIRS

I was 17 years old, and in my junior year at Highland Park when I signed up for the On Job Training (O.J.T.) program. The program paid for, and allowed high school students to leave campus to receive on the job training in a specific trade and earn college credits. I was in limbo in terms of what career I wanted to pursue, and had to face the reality that I would not be going to the NBA. I wanted to choose something that had purpose, something I was passionate about, but that would make me some money. At first I was interested in becoming a mechanic like my dad and my uncles, but that was short lived. Then it dawned on me, why not do something that I loved doing, which was cutting hair, and making people look and feel good? So, I entered the Cosmetology program instead, hoping to earn my credentials as a certified cosmetologist. I began taking courses part-time at Saint Paul College while going to high school, and giving haircuts in the basement.

I had been cutting hair since I was 11 years old and had taken over as the barber of the family. In my personal opinion, I had already perfected every type of haircut, style and design imaginable. My clipper game was strong, and my lineups were superb. I had the whole neighborhood raving about how clean my fades were. The basement barbershop had been bustling for years by that point. My clientele spoke for itself. I had the game on lock!

After graduating from Highland Park, the O.J.T. program no longer paid my tuition, and I needed to find a way to make money to remain in the cosmetology program. I started cutting hair full-time in the basement, and had a few side hustles while still attending Saint Paul College. I worked extremely hard to put myself in a financial position to fund the start of my career as a cosmetologist. I paid my tuition out of my own pocket, along with my books, supplies, and everything else I needed, without taking out any financial aide or student loans. I used the money I had accumulated from cutting in the basement and the many other side hustles I had at the time. Some of them were legit, and some were not so much. I couldn't afford to take any penitentiary chances. I was on my grind! My dream was to ultimately open up my own hair salon. I had the clientele, but first, I needed to earn my credentials.

After my first semester, I found out that cosmetology was much different and more difficult than I had originally thought. My instructor told me, "You will never make it in this industry if you only cut hair. You will need to learn how to do manicures, pedicures, and facials if you want to become a cosmetologist."

I thought to myself, I don't need to deal with this mess, and considered dropping out. Then, I remembered the lessons I had learned along the way and why I had decided to enter the cosmetology program in the first place. More than anything, I wanted to open up my own salon, and knew I needed that piece of paper to do it. I was already nearly a master barber in terms of skills, and experience. But, I had this instructor that had no idea the sacrifices that I had made to put myself in this position. I should be teaching her, I thought. I had come this far, and there was no turning back now. So I pressed on. I asked myself, "What are you willing to do to achieve what it is you want to accomplish in life?"

I was on the cusp of becoming a certified cosmetologist. This was another defining moment that had the potential to shift the trajectory of my life. My future depended on it.

Similar to my experience on the basketball court, there are moments when the momentum shifts, and the opposing team goes on a run. You can either get down on yourself, start pointing fingers at your teammates, your coach, or who- ever. You cannot let anything break your mental focus, and you must keep your eyes on the prize. There is a goal to accomplish. I had to worry about the things I could control. I knew what I came here to do, and I wasn't about to let any- body or anything stop me! I damn sure wasn't going to be the one to stop myself. This was *my* time! It was all about how I responded. So I kept my foot on the gas—All gas, no breaks!

While I was attending Saint Paul College, an opportunity presented itself that would allow me to cut hair in a shop for the first time. A barber named Mack owned a shop on Selby Avenue and Milton Street, and he recently got locked up. The manager's name was Goody, and he hired me to cut hair for a month until Mack came home from jail. I made $1,000 a week.

Another barber named Mr. Dee had a shop on Selby Avenue and Dale Street beside Till- man's market, right next to a vacant lot, which was within walking distance from my house. I would walk or ride my bike to his shop while I was still in high school, up until I got my cosme- tology license, and he would pay me to cut his hair on Fridays. After I graduated he was in need of a barber, and that's when Mr. Dee hired me to cut hair at his shop. This was in 1996, around the time Amy and I started dating again. Her parents lived right behind Mr. Dee's shop, and I would stop by to see her after work.

While at cosmetology school, I met another barber named Omar who had similar dreams and aspirations as me. We both shared the dream of opening up our own shop, and would talk about our vision during class. Together, we planned to take over the Twin Cities. Because he graduated after me, our plans were put on hold until one day he called me up, and told me he was starting his own business and wanted me to partner with him. We put our heads together and decided he would own the shop, while I managed the shop. The idea was genius!

After graduating, we created a business plan, and opened our own all purpose hair salon called Ennovations, spelled with an E. The dream was coming to fruition! Business was good, and we had established our reputation and a solid foundation to build on. However, the dream was deferred, and abruptly turned to a nightmare. The older heads who owned the building sold it and gave us a 30 day notice to vacate the premises. We were devastated, and now forced to go our separate ways to find work.

After leaving Ennovations, I moved around the city to a few different shops in Saint Paul. First, I went over to Eric Townsends shop on the East Side, off Arcade Street and Sims Avenue, across the street from Rainbow Foods. Then I moved to Goody's shop located on the corner of Rice Street, and Atwater Avenue. I was just starting to get comfortable when a series of unfortunate events occurred that left me stranded on an island. It felt like I was walking through nothing but revolving doors…In reality, it was a part of the game—more like a game of revolving chairs.

After a year of cutting at the shop, Goody sold the barbershop to a guy named S.P., who was a friend and one of our fellow barbers. A few more years passed, and the culture at the shop began to shift from positive to negative in subtle ways. My clients were loyal, and we had a mutual respect for one another despite some of their transgressions outside of the chair. As I had said before, the chair was a safe space. But you couldn't always control who came into the barbershop, nor discriminate against anybody who is in need of a haircut. There were moments where different people brought different energy, and that could shift a good vibe, if you know what I mean.

I remember it was the early winter of 2001 during Thanksgiving break, because my son Rob J was born that December. Another barber's client purchased a vehicle from S.P. who was now the owner. The man supposedly wanted his money back, and a verbal confrontation took place between him and S.P. Later, someone apparently went over to S.P.'s house, pulled out a gun and started shooting. S.P. had gotten shot!

Everything was on pause, and the shop was closed. Meanwhile, the Saint Paul police were investigating and ended up raiding the barbershop. Later on, I found out that the police had taken my appointment book, which had all my client contacts in it. I called the police station to inquire about the whereabouts of my appointment book, and they informed me that it had been taken as evidence, and they'd mail it back to me. Eventually, I received my appointment book in the mail.

Things were getting wild, and I wasn't sure if S.P. was going to survive. Reality was setting in, and I had no option but to separate myself from the nonsense. Once again, I was out of work.

CHAPTER 6

NUMBERS DON'T LIE

Amy and I met at Highland Park Middle School. As teenagers, we were quite immature but were attracted to each other like magnets, and had established a deep connection. We began dating our sophomore year, and often talked about getting married, having kids and buying a house together. You know that happily ever after type shit. Like most teenage love affairs, things got a little too serious; and like most young men do to girls they really cared about, I broke things off. It wasn't until we both graduated from high school, and I finished the cosmetology program at Saint Paul College that our paths crossed again, and we circled back around.

It was 1996, and as I mentioned previously, the first shop that I ever worked at was Mr. Dee's and Amy's parents lived directly behind the shop. There's no such thing as coincidence. One day, I decided to stop by. I knocked on the back door, and her Father answered. He said to Amy "Some dingbat is at the door," and then she came downstairs.

Amy and I picked up right where we left off. Like I said, the connection had long been established, and we instantaneously got back together. Nevertheless, she was intelligent, witty, had good energy, and was fun to be around. I was attracted to her personality, not to mention she was beautiful. Our relationship grew every minute, every hour, every day, and every year, and evolved into an unconditional love that I never imagined. She was and still is my best friend, and a cornerstone in my life. They say that if you like it, then you should put a ring on it. Uh oh!

In 1998, Amy and I got engaged to be married. We were in our early twenties, and each decided that we would each get physicals prior to us getting married. Her physical exam went well, and she passed with flying colors, while mine showed some abnormalities in terms of my kidney function. I thought nothing of it, as I was in pristine physical shape, and had played basketball my entire life, worked out regularly, all while standing on my feet for hours each day cutting hair. Nonchalantly, the doctor said that they'd watch it.

I thought nothing of it.

I had finally finished the cosmetology program at Saint Paul College, and earned my certification. I was checking off boxes, and building a solid foundation for my future. I had transitioned from cutting in the basement to Mr. Dee's, and then helped open up Ennovations. Once I moved to Goody's barbershop off Rice Street, the money was flowing like the Mississippi. Amy and I had jumped the broom, and decided to buy a house together. It was a beautiful single family, two story, with metal siding on Birmingham Street in a low key neighborhood on the east side of Saint Paul.

Amy was pregnant with our first son when I started to experience some increased back pain and concerns regarding my health. Nothing major in my opinion at the time, but enough to where Amy recommended I make a doctor's appointment. My previous physical showed that my creatinine levels were slightly higher than normal, but I was feeling just fine up until that point.

I had been experiencing some headaches, and some minor aches and pains. One day, my in-laws, a few friends, and I were building a garage in the back of my house. We took a break and went to get everybody some Burger King.

All of the sudden my head started pounding, and I had the worst headache that I had ever experienced. It felt like my head was going to explode! It was to the point where Amy suggested that we pause on the garage, and continue another day. I went into the bedroom and sat on the bed, and rocked back and forth. It got so bad that Amy took me to the doctor the following day.

They referred me to what would've been my third nephrologist by this time. So, we met with the nephrologist and they took some more urine samples. The nephrologist asked me again if I had ever peed blood, which I had. I got every test you could possibly think of. They analyzed my blood samples, and tested my creatinine levels to assess my kidney function.

So, we went in to see my current nephrologist. They ran more tests, took more blood samples, and tested my creatinine level again. The doctor told me that my body gave off a scent that my kidneys were bad…A *scent,* I thought…What type of scent? We waited for them to come back, and tell us what my creatinine levels were.

When the nephrologist walked back into the room, he said to me, "Your creatinine level is extremely high." Most people started dialysis at a creatinine level of ten. My creatinine level was nearly doubled, and was sitting at 19.5. The doctor told me that, "what you're actually experiencing is kidney failure."

I was in denial and said "Ok, what is that supposed to mean?"

The doctor responded, and said "You're a walking deadman. People don't walk around and *live* with numbers that high."

The numbers said that I needed a kidney. He went on to inform me that what I was experiencing was kidney failure, and that I would need a transplant in the near future. I looked him in the eye, and thought he must be crazy!

They kept telling me that my numbers were saying that I should be on dialysis. I was in shock! My mind started racing, and I'm staring off into space.

I was going to need a kidney.

I was in my early twenties, why would I need a kidney? I wasn't comprehending what was going on. They were saying that my numbers were high but in comparison to how I was feeling, it made no sense to me.

"Robert, you need to go on dialysis before it's *too* late." the doctor said.

I thought, too late?!

"What do you mean before it's too late?" I said. The doctor looked at me as if he was staring deep into my soul.“*Too late.*” he emphasized.

I remember being distraught, and in pure disbelief as Amy and I walked out of the nephrology clinic. Feeling defeated, I dropped into the passenger seat of the car, reclined my seat, and closed my eyes as tears streamed down my cheeks.

I was consumed with the thought that I was going to die.

Wait, I *couldn't* die!

My thoughts started racing. Amy was 5 months pregnant. We already decided that Amy was going to leave her job, and be a stay at home Mom.

“Was I going to live to see the birth of my son?”

That was the longest drive home ever.

CHAPTER 7

TRUST THE PROCESS

I needed dialysis before it was too late, and it hit me like a ton of bricks. Suddenly, I was carrying so much weight, and the pressure was insurmountable. Everything that I had planned to do was now put on hold, and I was forced to pick up the fragmented pieces of my shattered dreams. It was the story of my life!

It felt like I was running a relay race. I'd get close to the finish line, my dreams just an arm's length away. I'd stretch out my arms just enough to touch it, and stumble. My legs would give out. Whether it was my hoop dreams, or Ennovations, there always seemed to be these external forces acting as a barrier between me and the manifestation of my dreams. I went from building a garage to end-stage kidney failure, to needing to go on dialysis. Everything was flipped upside down!

Amy was five months pregnant with our first kid. What could I do?

At my nephrology appointment the doctor created an intensive treatment plan, and I started dialysis a week later. The first step was to be admitted to United Hospital where they would insert the catheter in my chest. They also gave me my first few dialysis treatments and monitored me for a week to ensure that my body responded accordingly.

My friend Tony Jefferson, Amy and my Mom came to visit me in the hospital. Tony looked at me like Superman's down, and I knew I was in bad shape. When I left the hospital, I was able to return to work a few days later. The nephrologist put me on a treatment schedule, which required me to go to Davita Dialysis Center in Maplewood three days a week.

I remember walking into my first dialysis treatment at Davita, and I was scared to death. It felt and looked like walking into an infirmary. There were several dialysis patients laying in recliners, hooked up to machines, and all of them were waiting on kidney transplants. No offense but the dialysis patients looked half dead. I assumed that I looked the same way. I asked the receptionist where the bathroom was, and they told me it was down the hallway on my right. I walked in, looked in the mirror, and started to shed tears. I splashed some water on my face, and I remember telling myself to get it together, that I could do this. Shit, I had to do this! After I got my mind right, I stepped out of the bathroom and approached the receptionist's desk.

They introduced me to my dialysis technician, and I sat down in an open recliner chair. They connected me, and the machine started pumping. It sounded like it was humming. I vividly remember sinking down into the chair, and closing my eyes in disbelief of what transpiring. It was all good just a week ago.

I was cutting Tuesday through Saturday, while still going to dialysis Monday, Wednesday and Friday. On Wednesdays and Fridays, I'd be on my feet cutting until 2pm, then go to dialysis afterwards. I wouldn't get home until 7pm or later. Then I'd wake up early on Tuesday, Thursday, and Saturday and cut all day for 9-10 hours. I'd be in the shop late, sometimes even after hours.

Thinking back, it is crazy that I was able to maintain cutting and dialysis, considering how invasive dialysis treatment was on my body. The dialysis machine called a dialyzer removed and filtered my blood through a catheter in my chest, and cleaned out the toxins that my kidneys could no longer remove. The filtered blood was then returned to my body. While I was connected to the machine, all I could do was just lay there. The whole process would leave me extremely weak.

I had a certified dialysis technician, and just like any field of service there are people that truly care and those that don't. Certain techs treated me differently, and I had a different technician every time, so each treatment session was a roll of the dice.

After it was determined that I needed a kidney transplant, the entire family, including my mom, dad and my siblings lined up like who's it going to be? All of them got tested and were willing to give up a part of themselves for me to live. My sister Angie wanted to be the one to save my my life but was pregnant at the time so she was excluded. She felt helpless, and that triggered the same feeling she had when I almost drowned in the swimming pool when we were kids. She was devastated. My brother Ronnie was still in high school, and too young at the time so it couldn't be him. That left my mom, dad and my brother Reggie. My mom and dad had already sacrificed so much for us. Although, I needed a kidney to live, I didn't want my parents to have to donate.

When it came to Reggie, I was always the one responsible for my little brother's safety and it was my job to protect him. Still he stepped up, took the test and it was determined that he was a perfect match. The doctor stated that it seemed as if we were twins. However, there was a donor list and although he was a perfect match, they placed him on the waiting list of potential donors. I needed to play the waiting game. I had to *trust the process.*

Months of being on dialysis had taken its toll on me. At times I felt like throwing in the towel and questioned whether or not it was worth the amount of daily pain I was in. But these were the cards that I was dealt, and I couldn't fold my hand. If it wasn't for my wife and unborn child, I probably would've tapped out, but I still had so much to live for. There was just so much pressure and unpredictability in those days, and it made me question if the treatment was even worth it.

I had many dark moments on dialysis because of what it did to my body. Each time that I did dialysis I'd lose approximately 10 pounds, and on the days I didn't go, I had to limit the amount of water I drank because I would retain fluid. For instance, if I went to dialysis, and I was retaining fluid, I would need to go in for an additional treatment on Saturday. This left my body feeling depleted. The side effects made me extremely dehydrated, and caused my body to severely cramp up. It also caused me to feel dizzy, and while at work I'd often have to go home for the day, especially when I felt nauseous or started vomiting. On dialysis, I could only drink a limited amount of water in a 24 hour time frame, and I'd be extremely thirsty.

Fluid retention was extremely common and would happen to me constantly. If the dialysis treatment wasn't pulling enough toxins out, the excess fluid would go to my arms, legs, and testicles. The fluid caused my balls to swell up to the size of a cantaloupe. If I had to shit, I would have to lift my balls up, otherwise they would touch the toilet water. I would then have to piss in a cup or bucket. My balls swelled up multiple times while I was on dialysis, and the longest it lasted was 2-3 weeks. I still worked in that condition, and wore briefs to support my swollen testicles and would have to walk extremely slow.

I remember going to the doctor for an examination. I pulled down my pants, and asked the doctor if the swelling was normal. The doctors told me that it was. I asked them if there was anything they could do, and they told me all I could do was wait. They also didn't give me anything for the pain. So, I endured the pain, and just waited for it to get drained off at dialysis. At night, I hardly slept because of the unbearable pain, and the constant need to adjust them. There were times I felt like I was going to die from all the fluid retention.

Most of my clients had no idea what I dealt with on a daily basis. In between clients I'd take breaks by sitting down in a chair. There were times that I'd have to reschedule my client's appointments depending on what side effects I had from the dialysis treatment and the medications I was taking.

I remember one time I had to reschedule my appointments because I needed to go home for the day. As I was getting ready to leave, one of my clients showed up anyway and still wanted his hair cut. I explained to him that I wasn't feeling well and couldn't cut, and was waiting to be picked up. He said, "you're still here aren't you?" and demanded that I cut him anyway. Some clients just didn't understand.

Everyday when I walked through those doors to get treatment, I wondered what was going to happen that day. Was I going to pass out? Was I going to have to go to the hospital? Was I going to leave my car here? Was I not going to be able to go home tonight? Was I not going to be able to go to work tomorrow? Was I going to feel like shit? Which I probably was…Was I going to be able to go home and do what I needed to do? There was just so many things that ran through my brain. It felt like I had aged years, and everything was so painful. It got to the point where I just refused the meds. A lot of times the pain meds they gave me made me feel worse.

After one of my dialysis treatments, I felt like I was going to pass out. As I left dialysis, I told myself that I needed some exercise, and instead of taking the elevator, I decided to take the stairs down to the parking lot. An older man was standing by the door to the stairwell, waiting for his wife to finish dialysis. As I opened the door to enter the stairwell, he stopped me, and we started talking. As we talked my hearing began going in and out, so I turned toward one of the technicians nearby, and told her that I thought I was going to pass out. The next thing I remember is sitting in one of the dialysis chairs, the technicians lifting my feet up and feeding me butterfingers. I have always thought about that day, and wondered what would've happened if that man hadn't stopped me. Would I have passed out in the stairwell? What would've happened to me then? God always seems to send the right people at the right time.

You often hear about the small percentage of people who experienced side effects of medications and medical treatments, and that 99% of people didn't experience side effects. I was that 1% that did. I seemed to experience every side effect that dialysis had to offer. Dialysis felt like I was wearing a band-aide; it temporarily stopped the bleeding, but the wound never healed. It turned into a tumultuous relationship that felt like a never ending cycle. At least until I received a kidney transplant. Everyday was getting harder. My mind, body and spirit started to break down. There seemed to be this reoccurring theme in my life of needing to *trust the process*.

I was trapped in survival mode at this point in my life. I had to find a way to stay focused on the grind, and try not to feed into the thought of not being there for the birth of my first son. I felt like I failed as a husband, in terms of having the ability to support my wife. Between cutting hair and going to dialysis I was depleted. I was mentally, physically and spiritually drained, and emotionally unavailable. I needed a break!

While I was home for Thanksgiving, I received the news that S.P. was shot and it added another layer to the stress. Luckily, he lived, but was in critical condition, and so was the shop. Shortly after the shooting the police raided the shop and it was shut down, and suddenly I was out of work. That same weekend on December 1st, Amy went into labor and I witnessed the birth of my son, Robert Junior. Thank you God!

It was one of the most beautiful moments of my life when I witnessed my son come into the world. A star was born…Unfortunately, after I held him for the first time, I had to rush to dialysis and didn't get to stay with my family. That was a bittersweet feeling. But I was blessed! I no longer had to question whether or not I would lay eyes on my first born son. Amy and I fell in love all over again with the start of our family.

Speaking of family, I had close friends that worked at Backstage barbershop. They informed me that the owner Pam was looking for a barber. I met with Pam to discuss the opportunity, and a few weeks later, I started cutting at Backstage. Pam was aware that I needed a kidney and was undergoing dialysis. She understood my health issues and supported me when I needed to go to dialysis.

The environment at Backstage was positive and a nice change of pace. It gave me a fresh new start. She also supported my dream of opening up my own spot, and we agreed that my time there would be temporary. Regardless, backstage felt like home and would be for the foreseeable future.

After six months of working at Backstage, we got a phone call from the doctors. There was a cancellation and we got moved up on the donor waiting list. The date was set for my transplant, and soon I would no longer need dialysis. I was in disbelief that they had moved the date up and that my kidney donor would be my brother Reggie! The news left me excited but left Reggie with an enormous amount of anxiety. He said to me "you're really about to take a piece of my body!" Reggie stated that leading up to that phone call, his spirit was speaking to him the entire time and he was feeling the pressure. It had been a long 11 months on dialysis and it would finally come to an end. I was getting a kidney!

I could barely sleep the night prior to the surgery and laid awake staring at the ceiling. It had been the longest 11 months of my life, and I was elated that I would not have to step foot into another dialysis office again. I had my bags packed and was prepared for my transplant as well as my recovery. Amy drove me to the hospital at about 3 AM so they could prep me for surgery and I walked confidently into the hospital. At last I was getting my kidney transplant.

Shortly after I arrived, Reggie pulled up in his Thunderbird and I could hear his 15's banging from inside my room. At first they had us both in separate rooms, but shortly afterwards wheeled us into the pre-operating room with our beds side-by-side. I could sense his fear and anxiety, but we started telling jokes and laughing. He said that he couldn't believe they were going to literally take out a piece of his body and give it to me. Reggie said that it felt like a scene from that Indiana Jones movie. We were getting ready to enter the temple of doom!

The doctors walked in, verified our charts, and asked us a few questions before prepping us for surgery. When we were getting put under anesthesia, it felt like we jumped into a rocket ship. We were buckled up and getting ready to go to another world. We started the countdown at *Ten… Nine… Eight… Sev…*and it all went silent and dark. Together in the same room side-by-side we took off on our journey. Never had we imagined that we'd be right here, right now. Our lives were in God's hands, and he held us close. If something was to happen, at least we were together.

When Reggie and I woke up from surgery, we were in a totally different place than when we went under. Not just location or room wise but mentally, physically and spiritually. It felt like the procedure was over in a blink of an eye, and we were lying there weak and vulnerable.

Reggie described it as an obstacle course, but we didn't know the obstacles would be that immense. The transplant took energy from his body and transferred it to my body. It was like he jump started my battery, but completely drained his. He was on empty and felt like he was on the verge of dying.

After a few days, I was feeling good and able to walk around the room. I was feeling happy and energetic, while Reggie was going through some things. He stared at me, then started hitting the nurse button for assistance. When the nurse walked in Reggie told them to take my happy ass out!

He wanted everyone to leave the room and needed some time alone to gather himself. He was vomiting on himself, and having complications with the incision site. Each time he threw up, it would rip the stitches causing him to bleed. He was going through it! Reggie said he felt a lot of emptiness and not just because they had removed one of his kidneys, but that it also took so much energy to heal. The recovery process for a kidney donation is brutal on your mind, body and soul. It literally sucked all your energy, even while you were sitting down. Your abdominal muscles would be so weak and just to sit up expended a large amount of energy. You'd be sitting in the same place for hours, and the little bit of energy that you did have needed to be used to walk a few steps to the bathroom or to make a sandwich. Things progressed and we got a little further each day. According to Reggie, it was the most humbling experience of his life. It took him an entire year to recover. It was a bumpy ride.

As far as my recovery went, I was able to walk around immediately afterwards, and had much more energy than I had while I was on dialysis. I was overjoyed and feeling good. I hadn't felt that good in a long time. After three days of them monitoring my kidney, my body was responding really well, so I was able to try solid food. The nurse gave me a meal that included broccoli. That was a bad idea! I'm not sure why they decided to give me broccoli because it caused a large amount of gas in my stomach. The gas caused me so much pain, constipation and bloating that I was screaming uncontrollably.

I screamed so loud that Reggie could hear me from his room on the other end of the hallway. The nurses had to give me an enema and laxatives to relieve the gas and constipation. After five days, I felt better and they sent me home. I had a second chance at life.

CHAPTER 8

BACK IN THE PIT

A few months after the kidney transplant, I returned to Backstage and was embraced by Pam, Wesley, Mark Dog and my clients. My clients remained loyal, and soon after my return, my spirit and appointment book were full again. The connections I had built over the years were stronger than ever, and it was a testament to my dedication and ability to bounce back. I had clients that stayed with me through thick and thin, many from as far back as the basement and many who followed me from shop to shop. Looking back on my career up until that point, I realized that I was making an impact on the community solely by cutting hair.

My clients consisted of multiple generations, and I cut entire families that included grandparents, mothers and fathers, and their children. The expression on a parent's face when they witnessed their child getting their first haircut is priceless. These were milestones in both of our lives. I would give them a certificate and a small portion of their hair to take home after their first cut. Cutting children has been one of the most rewarding and fulfilling aspects of becoming a barber. A fresh haircut doesn't just alter a person's appearance; it infused them with confidence and pride, and giving them positive self-esteem and a sense of identity.

The environment at Backstage was beautiful and each day brought its share of characters and personalities. There was a guy who walked in with the knockoff sunglasses, gold watches and every cologne you could think of. There was the bootleg man who had all the movies and DVD's you needed. There was a culture that was built at Backstage, and it was a special place that was near and dear to my heart. The jokes and laughter were just as common as the consultations that took place in the chair. I wasn't only a barber, I was a counselor, therapist and life coach to so many folks. They also provided the same for me at times, and the human connection is something I cannot emphasize enough. Backstage was a special place.

For the five to six years after my kidney transplant, Backstage was like a second home to me. I was grateful to have had the support from Pam, my fellow barbers, and my community during that time. After five years a lot had changed for the better and some for the worst. Mark Dog got locked up and for a brief period there was an open chair, and only two barbers, Brandon and myself cutting hair. Soon afterward, Kandis joined the Backstage team, and they each became part of my extended family. Without them I wouldn't be where I was today.

Around this time, I went to my monthly blood draw to ensure my creatinine levels were stable, and my kidney was functioning properly. At one of my monthly blood draws, my blood test showed that my creatinine levels were slightly higher than normal and sitting between 4-5 mg/dl. My nephrologist recommended plasmapheresis as a precaution to avoid kidney rejection. Plasmapheresis was a similar process as my dialysis treatment. It was similar as in I had to get the catheter inserted in the exact part of my chest as I did when I needed dialysis. Instead of filtering my blood, it was cleaning the plasma in my body to promote my kidney's health and decrease my creatinine level. Plasmapheresis was also extremely painful and I attended treatment three days a week for a month. My nephrologist said that the kidney responded well, my creatinine levels had dropped, and my body was feeling amazing.

It had been a solid nine years since my first kidney transplant and I was feeling stronger than ever. I was going on a decade plus of cutting hair at Back Stage, and was starting to feel that itch again of opening up my own shop. Back Stage was a good situation, and the other barbers and I had such a strong bond. But I still had dreams and aspirations of my own shop. I had to scratch that itch!

By this time, I had three children Rob J, Amber and Devan. Everything was moving in the right direction, and I was in a position to start making some power moves for my career as a barber, an entrepreneur, and a family man. I started looking for potential spots to purchase, but nothing met my standards. I planned to take my time and make sure that when I made that move it wouldn't put me in the same situation as what had happened with Ennovations. Either I was going to own the building out right, or it would be a spot that was secure and sustainable for the future. I had options, and wasn't going to rush.

Nine years after my kidney transplant, I had gotten severely sick with something similar to the flu, and was extremely ill. I just remember being slumped over, and severely weak. A friend of mine drove me to the nephrology clinic to see my kidney doctor, who referred me back to my primary doctor. They took a chest x-ray, and believed that I had walking pneumonia, and thought I needed antibiotics. My doctor called my nephrologist, and I heard them talking about how to treat my illness. Together they decided to prescribe me a medication I had never taken before, which was an antibiotic called Augmentin. Normally, they would prescribe me a Z-pack, so this felt a little odd. I had that gut feeling and my intuition was telling me that something wasn't right, but I ignored it. What they prescribed me caused me to vomit, and have diarrhea excessively. I couldn't hold anything down, and that dehydrated my kidney.

After seven days of being in this condition I went to the hospital. I stayed there for a week and they couldn't figure out what was wrong, so they sent me home. Another week had passed and it was still occurring, so I went back to the hospital. After three weeks of having diarrhea and vomiting, they informed me that I was having side effects to the medication, which is a condition called C-diff. They ran some tests to determine if I indeed had C-diff, but the tests came back negative. Still, they treated me as if I had C-diff, and my condition improved. However, by that point the Augmentin had destroyed my transplanted kidney. I was *back in the pit again*!

The doctors told me I had to go back on dialysis. I was instantly triggered and could feel the trauma I had experienced during the first time I went through dialysis surging through my body. I started to break down! It was mentally, emotionally, and spiritually depleting. My brain was scrambled, and I was in one of the darkest places of my life.

Nine years after my kidney transplant, they reinserted the catheter in my chest and I started dialysis immediately. I was struggling for dear life, still vomiting and had diarrhea…They said I never had walking pneumonia, and I never found out why they gave me that antibiotic to begin with. What I did find out was that my body was rejecting the kidney that I had received from Reggie. Now I had to fight for my life again, and if I was going to survive, I would have to rise from the ashes like a phoenix. That was a tough pill to swallow, and I wasn't sure I had it in me.

This time I had three kids, and my daughter Amber's birthday was coming up in a few days. I was determined to make it home for her birthday party. They released me from the hospital, and I got home just in time for my daughter's birthday. I was a shell of a man, and people noticed, but deep down I knew who I was. I was just going through a really rough time. I was back in the pit, and it was deeper, and darker than ever before.

CHAPTER 9

TOUR GUIDE TO THE DARK SIDE

I had already been to the dark side and back once before. This time around, I spent fourteen months on dialysis and had sat through some of the darkest moments of my life. It had been ten years since my first transplant, and now I was set to receive my second kidney transplant. It had been Reggie who donated his kidney during the first transplant, and miraculously this time it would be my Dad who was chosen to donate a piece of himself for his son to live. It must've been divine intervention because not only was it rare to find somebody living to donate a kidney, but for it to be a family member it felt like it was meant to be.

Fortunately, because I had been through a kidney transplant before, I knew what to expect going into my second one. I was familiar with the recovery process, and knew the timeline in terms of the amount of days I could expect to be in the hospital. To avoid the standard five to seven days it took to recover, I started to prepare my body well in advance. So, I exercised to the best of my ability, did push-ups and sit-ups to get myself in shape. I challenged myself, and my goal was to be released from the hospital in two to three days max.

My dad had gone through the kidney screening process, and surprisingly passed despite being fifty seven years old at the time. He was brutally honest about his experiences on the planet, including his participation in recreational marijuana use. He said that if smoking a little weed was going to stop them from allowing him to give a kidney to his son, then he would raise hell. He wasn't as transparent about experimenting with morphine because he knew that would be a red flag. His intention for trying morphine had solely been about the understanding that after kidney transplant surgery, that's what the doctors were going to give you. My Dad had been curious as to how morphine would affect him and what it would do to his body.

He had a high tolerance for pain from his days of growing up in Mississippi. He told stories of stepping on rusty nails, accidentally cutting himself with knives, and the time he nearly chopped his toe off with an axe. Going under the knife gave him no cause for concern, and he firmly believed that God was on his side. He always said that you have to get in contact with your higher power. The way he looked at it was that if he were to die on that table, it would be an honorable death. He said to me, "What is more honorable than that?"

The power of faith was something that was very much understood in our family, and we believed that this was something we were being called to do. Sometimes in life, you were called to do things you didn't fully understand. Between me, my dad and Reggie, we each did a lot of soul searching. We had to have conviction! Reggie said that this was what separated the men from the boys. It was time to ride for our family! Our spirits were connected and we shared a universal power. Apparently, we also shared kidneys.

My dad and I tried to make light out of a heavy situation by telling jokes and laughing together prior to the procedure. I remember when the doctor walked in, he peeked at our charts, and then said to my dad, "It looks like you're getting a kidney today." We looked at each other like, is he serious? Does he know what is going on? My dad quickly corrected him, but it was unsettling. I wasn't sure if, it was because my dad was older, the doctor thought I was the one giving him my kidney, but we brushed it off. We laughed, and joked about me having three kidneys but not one of them working.

As funny as that was, it added to the fear and anxiety we had going in. Little did we know that would only be the beginning.

They gave us each a pre-op medication, and prepped us both for anesthesia. I wasn't sure exactly what type of medication they gave me, but almost immediately it made my throat feel itchy. I asked the nurse to get the doctor, and expressed that something was wrong, but they disregarded my concerns. The doctor never came back into the room, and all I remember is seeing the lights along the ceiling as they pushed me down the hallway toward the operating room.

They were having trouble locating my dad's vein, so they brought in a vein specialist for my dad. From what he said, he had no idea they had injected him with the anesthesia. Before he went under, they hadn't given him the countdown, and in a split second, he woke up confused and delirious. When he opened his eyes, he realized the surgery was over and they had removed his kidney. The bed was trembling as if he was on a rocket ship, and the pressure of the pain was so intense that he was shaking uncontrollably; he also realized he couldn't speak. Reggie called it going into the pain pit, and one of the rules of the pain pit was that you were unable to speak.

My dad explained to me that when you wake up, it was like being in the Alfred Hitchcock film series, The Breakdown. The scene when the man was laying on the hospital bed, while the doctors hovered over him believing he was dead. The man had his eyes wide open; he could hear, and feel the pain but couldn't move or speak, and with tears rolling down his cheeks, he laid there helpless. The doctors believed the man to be dead and wheeled him into the icebox where they stored the dead bodies.

My dad said that he heard the doctors say that he wasn't breathing! Mind you, he is unable to communicate and couldn't simply say that he *was* breathing. He started to panic! Then he remembered that during the kidney donor orientation, they advised him that when he came out of surgery to take short breaths. So, he said to himself, start taking short breaths, short breaths, short breaths. Finally, the doctors said loudly, "He's breathing!"

These are the experiences that Reggie, my Dad and I described as being in between worlds. It was that gray space where it felt like your spirit was separate from your body. Very similar to how I felt when I nearly drowned in that swimming pool as a kid. It was like you were there but also in some type of alternate parallel universe. These were the moments that surpassed our human comprehension. Maybe it was the drugs they had given us, but from our perspective, it was like we were existing in another dimension;

the dimension between life and death. My Dad called it the crossroads. Many people who had near-death experiences often described this realm as a purgatory of sorts, and not to impose any religious beliefs on anyone, but our God was with us. Without our faith, we wouldn't have gotten through the pain, through the suffering, or through the entire process of the kidney transplantation journey. We had to jump over this last hurdle and get through this final stretch, which was to endure the pain of healing. This was how it had to happen!

When I woke from surgery, I was in the most excruciating pain of my life. It felt like I had been hit by a train traveling at tremendous speed, and my entire body had been crushed. I heard the distant chatter of the doctors and nurses conversing in the background, but couldn't make out exactly what they were saying. One of them said something about an allergic reaction. I thought to myself, they couldn't be talking about me. Then I recalled that before I went into surgery, I tried communicating to the nurses to call the doctor because my throat felt weird after they gave me the pre-op medication but they didn't listen!

Then I heard a flip of a light switch, and was startled by the flash of light. I tried to open my eyes but couldn't. The light was so bright it was like trying to stare directly at the sun and I couldn't see! It felt like I had wax paper over my eyelids. I reached for my wife's hand, and whispered her name. Amy…Somebody help! They're trying to kill me! Amy grabbed and held my hand, and assured me that it was going to be alright, and she was right there. She explained to me that I had an allergic reaction to the pre-op med, and they needed to reverse all the medication they'd given me for the pain. So, I woke up from my second kidney transplant without any morphine or pain medication in my body. Because my potassium was so high, they had to wait for it to drop before they could give me anything to counter the pain, otherwise my heart would've stopped!

I had a high pain tolerance, but this was a level of pain I've never experienced before. I'd also been through a kidney transplant procedure once before, and thought I knew what to expect going into the second one. But I never anticipated this! They were preparing to take me to the intensive care unit (I.C.U.), when my potassium finally dropped. It was finally at the point where they could give me morphine to decrease the pain.

Because of the complications that I experienced following my first kidney transplant procedure, I wanted to move with discretion when it came to medication. But this pain was surpassing my typical pain threshold. Following a kidney transplant, a majority of the soreness is located in your abdominal area. After nearly 2 days of unbearable pain they wanted to continue to give me morphine. But, the pain would not subside.

The doctors refused to run diagnostic tests to figure out exactly what was going on. I had blood in my urine bag and had been telling them for two days that something was wrong. I felt a bulge and a substantial amount of pain specifically on the right side of my abdominal area. They refused to listen to me advocating for myself and responded by saying that it was normal after a kidney transplant. I wouldn't take no for an answer! My intuition was strong, and gut feelings don't lie. There was no reason that I should have needed a walker to walk. There was no reason that I wasn't able to lift my right leg to step onto the scale. There was no reason that my abdomen was so swollen that it looked like I was pregnant and my stitches were stretching.

After my first transplant I was walking around without assistance. I told them this, but they refused to listen untill I started throwing up blood and they finally gave me an ultrasound. She put the gel on my stomach, and placed the transducer against the right side of my abdomen. She took one look at the monitor, dropped the transducer and rushed out of the room. I *tried* to tell them!

CHAPTER 10

MINOR SETBACK FOR A MAJOR COMEBACK

After the nurse rushed out of the room, she quickly returned with my doctor and they stood in a huddle and urgently deliberated while pointing at the monitor. I anxiously waited for them to communicate with me exactly what it was they found inside my body.

The doctor informed me that the swelling and the bulge on the right side of my abdomen was a blood clot sitting on top of my nerve, and it was located exactly where they placed the kidney. To remove the blood clot, they would immediately have to perform another surgery and go back through the incision site and remove the clot.

I couldn't catch a break! That triggered the feeling I've had a dozen times, and once again I thought I was literally going to die. They prepped me for what would turn out be my sixth surgery, and second in a three day span. Luckily, they were able to address the blood clot, and told me that it was only a minor setback but that I'd be fine.

However, I would have to start the recovery process all over again. I woke from the surgery with a large amount of fear and anxiety, but unlike the last time, I could see and was feeling much better than I did previously. I laid in the hospital bed for a few minutes to process what just happened and pinched myself to make sure I was alive and I *was* alive! I lifted up my sheets, and was able to lift my right leg, then said aloud, "Thank you God!"

The doctors said to me, "Maybe we should *listen* to you next time." Now that the second surgery was successful, the way I was looking at the situation was that this is just a *minor setback for a major comeback.*

When it comes to medical integrity, I strongly believe there is discrimination within the health care system and biases that medical staff hold when it comes to honoring the patient's voice and perspective. Many instances throughout my kidney transplant journey medical staff failed to listen to me and disregarded my voice on numerous occasions. I had some unbelievable doctors and nurses, as well as some who were careless and dismissive to me as their patient. If they don't listen to the patient they run the risk of having somebody die. Oftentimes, the patient knows their body better than the doctor does. For example, when they prescribed medication it's typically based on the condition, symptoms and what the patient is telling them. When they asked me how severe my pain was on a scale of one to ten, and I told them that it's a ten; they're supposed to prescribe me something for that ten. If the morphine is not working, it makes no sense to up the dose of the morphine. Shouldn't the doctors be listening to me and try to assess what was causing my pain?

CHAPTER 11

REBUILDING THE FOUNDATION

I spent 3 months recovering from my second kidney transplant and took some time away from cutting hair to spend quality time with my loved ones. I took a vacation and went on a cruise with my family, spending a lot of that time reflecting on my life and showing gratitude for the little things in life. I was lucky to have a support system that consisted of my family and friends, who really went all in when the chips were down. Several of them came together and decided to throw benefits and fundraisers to help pay for my kidney treatments, medical bills, and to help my family stay afloat during my recovery. I owed them the world. I must thank Jay, Mary and her sister Paula, Keys Cafe and Mancini's; and all those individuals for literally throwing us a life preserver; otherwise we would've drowned in the sea of bills that had accumulated from all the medical care I had received. I had to thank my wife Amy, who stood by my side through thick and thin, held down the kids, and raised them when I was too weak to carry my own weight. She did all the heavy lifting, and all I needed to do was survive…and *I* survived!

Now I just needed to rebuild the foundation, and get back to where I needed to be. It was time to get focused spiritually, physically, mentally and financially. Not to sound conceited or overly confident, but I was known as the best barber in Minnesota.

Physically I was getting into some of the best shape of my life and was back to working out and rebuilding my body. My goal was to come back stronger and more muscular than ever. Honestly, I wanted my body to resemble a defensive back, and look like a free safety in the National Football League. I felt like I was ready for that type of workout regimen.

I couldn't stress enough how important it was to take care of my mental health. Just as you exercise to build up your muscle and physical physique, the same intention has to go into building up your mind. The power of the mind is one of the most underrated components to living a quality lifestyle. Solving most of our daily problems was really mind over matter. Self-care was vital to my mental health, and was deeply connected to my spiritual health.

My spiritual journey had its share of ups and downs, and my faith in God carried me through those low moments; together we climbed out of the darkness. I told myself as a young kid that I was going to be rich and stop cutting hair at 40. That was *my* plan, but that wasn't God's plan. I only had so many summers left. Now it was time to build my financial health and get back on my feet. Life often throws curveballs, and when it does, you either step up to the plate and swing for the fences or you walk away in defeat with your head down. The latter was not an option. I had come this far on my journey, recovered from two kidney transplants, and felt like I couldn't take anything for granted. I wanted to maximize my potential and still had goals that hadn't been accomplished. Those goals remained: opening up my own spot, and having the autonomy to make my own decisions.

Cutting hair at Backstage was originally supposed to be a short term situation. While at Backstage, I started to get complacent, stagnant and was unable to grow. I felt that itch again to opening up my own spot and needed to take control of my future. Many factors played a part in me leaving Backstage. There was a new building manager, and came into the shop micromanaging the barbers, making things difficult for us and our clients, especially during the State Fair. The fair took place over a two-week span through Labor Day, which is one of the busiest days for barber shops because most kids started school the day after and needed a fresh haircut for their first day.

During the fair, he leased out the parking lot for fair parking and made some of my clients pay for parking just to get a haircut. It was hard enough to deal with the State Fair traffic, which affected my clients arriving to their appointments on time and caused me to get behind, inconveniencing our customers. Towards the end of me working at Backstage, Pam told the new building manager that we would not be open for Labor Day anymore. But I had keys to the shop and scheduled appointments to honor my commitment to my clients, which caused a conflict of interest. It was extremely frustrating.

One of the breaking points at Backstage occurred when there was a shooting outside in the parking lot that left bullet holes in the glass windows in the front of the shop. It wasn't just that there were bullet holes in the glass; the windows never got replaced. This spoke to the upkeep of the building, as there were holes in the sheet rock, broken vending machines, and a general lack of care for the barbershop. It was time for me to move on! It was at that point that I started looking for my own spot.

I established Nabors Cut as a Limited Liability Company (LLC) shortly before leaving Backstage. I inquired about a few places in Roseville, and Saint Paul, one being Sola Salons. I received flyers in the mail from them regularly, and Amy suggested I schedule a meeting with them. They had different locations, one being on Hague Street near Mr. Dee's old shop in Saint Paul. It was a small, older building, and not exactly what I was looking for. After meeting with Sola Salons, they offered me my own studio and mentioned they were building a brand new location across the street from Maplewood Mall on White Bear Avenue. We went to go see it while it was still under construction; it didn't even have flooring yet—just gravel and dirt. However, it was a beautiful brand new building with a modern feel and a prime location. They showed me what studio would potentially be mine, which was a larger unit, and immediately I could envision exactly what I wanted my shop to look like. I knew it was the right decision. That day, I signed my contract, established a partnership with Sola Salons, and fulfilled my dream of opening up my own shop.

I planned to put in my two weeks' notice at Backstage and wanted to find a way to show my gratitude and thank Pam for taking me in and supporting me for the past fourteen and a half years. I met her in the hallway and asked if I could take her out to eat because I needed to talk to her about something. She immediately said to me, "You're leaving aren't you?" I responded that I would rather talk about it over lunch where I would explain more. But she declined, saying to just let her know when I was leaving so she could have somebody fill the chair. She walked away as I stood there in the hallway. I left the conversation thinking, "That's it? Right then I knew I was making the right decision. That was the beginning of Nabors Cut.

CHAPTER 12

BEYOND BARS

I signed a contract with the Ramsey County Adult Detention Center (A.D.C.) that led to a partnership with the Juvenile Detention Center (J.D.C.) while I was still working at Backstage. I developed a relationship through a childhood friend who lived across the street from me on Sherburne, and worked as a correctional officer (C.O.) at Boys Totem Town in Saint Paul. She introduced me to the opportunity to provide haircuts to incarcerated youth. I was contracted to provide haircuts to children ages 12-17, but I saw this as an opportunity to provide mentorship.

Many of the young men that I met came from broken homes, lacked positive male role models, made poor decisions, and succumbed to peer pressure. Most were unconsciously seeking guidance in their lives. Following my father's teachings, I used the barber chair as a space to talk to them about life, helping them unpack the reasons why they were locked up, and showing them how to transform their negative experiences into something positive. I wanted them to understand that it wasn't too late for them to turn their lives around. My goal was for them to leave upon release equipped with tools and an understanding of how to avoid returning to confinement. If a person can learn self discipline and channel their energy into something constructive, the sky's the limit.

It's all about the mindset. When you're institutionalized, it's not just your body that's locked up; your mind is too. It can be challenging to visualize a life beyond your current circumstances. Moreover, when you're incarcerated, it's not just you who suffers; your family and loved ones are doing time alongside you.

One young man I cut hair for was only 15 years old, had no father figure and a turbulent relationship with his mother He faced numerous challenges at home and school and was deeply involved in the streets. At just 12 years old, he and a group of friends decided to steal a car and rob someone at gunpoint. Long story short, he got caught, was arrested multiple times, and spent years institutionalized in J.D.C. While incarcerated, he became a father to a newborn baby boy, missing the birth and not meeting his son until he was released. His incarceration deeply affected his entire family, causing harm to his son, mother and sister.

Most of the kids I met in J.D.C. wanted to talk more but had to return to their pods or cells after getting their hair cut. When they walked into the room, and saw me setting up with my branded equipment, they often thought, oh he got money! I would respond by explaining that I didn't have a lot of money; what I did have, I reinvested in myself. While my gear might suggest wealth, the truth is that I returned it all to my business.

One of my clients who I had been cutting since childhood, was now locked up, awaiting trial for involvement in the murder of another client over a bag of weed. The gentleman who was killed had just graduated, started his own business and launched a clothing line. We had planned to collaborate, but before we could fulfill that commitment, he was shot and killed over something senseless.

Other inmates would sit in the chair, and as I threw the cape around them and began cutting their hair, they'd momentarily forget they were locked up. After the haircut, I'd hand them the mirror, spin them around, and watch them smile. But once that cape was removed, they'd return to their harsh reality of heading back to their cells.

In truth, we're all just one bad decision, one traffic stop, one cop having a bad day, or one drink away from jail. However, that doesn't mean we're all bad people. Before finding our purpose and having a chance to grow, we can be institutionalized. It's a recurring cycle many of us face, often unnoticed until it's too late. Yet, if we can slow down and communicate, we can open our eyes to different perspectives. At that age, I never thought about questions like: What am I doing? Where am I going? Who is at home? Who are my peers? What am I surrounding myself with? Regardless of age, these are questions everyone must ask themselves.

I wanted to create some type of outreach program—a group or classroom—where kids could gain an early advantage in life. A place to learn skills that would help them navigate the world. Too many children absorb messages from the music, television and social media without realizing that many of their idols are not living the lifestyles they portray; they are playing roles that are not true. This media programming leads them to speak, act and behave in ways that are detrimental to their lives. The media often depicts Black and Brown people as the most violent people, and if they remain unaware, they perpetuate these stereotypes, harming themselves in the process.

For me this work is not just about providing therapy for them; it's also therapy for me. I've said on the news that it's healing to help people feel and look good. When someone loves how they look and feel, it reflects back on me, confirming that I'm doing the right thing. I was committed to providing a service that helps them recognize their own humanity and envision a life beyond the bars.

CHAPTER 13

CREATE THE WEB

I coined the phrase "Create The Web" to capture my vision for the future after opening my own barbershop and hair salon. This concept represents an interconnected network woven together by my family, friends, and entrepreneurial experiences. It includes my newly established barbershop at Sola Salons, many of my clients, and individuals from all walks of life. "Create The Web" is focused on spiritual, mental, physical, and financially growth.

I think of it like a spider, which intentionally weaves a safety net, to protect, provide, and teach others in a sustainable and inspiring way. The spider's creativity and experience allow it to adapt to any circumstance, feeling at home no matter where the spider goes.

In 2017, I organized my first "Thanks 4 Giving" event at McDonough Recreation Center near the McDonough projects. The neighborhood is a highly impoverished, with families and children needing assistance during the holiday season. We wanted to give back directly to the people in need. Together as the Nabors family, we organized and strategized to hold an annual event near Thanksgiving. We brought together community members, activists, barbers, hair stylists, youth workers, organizations. We provided free haircuts, hair braiding, face painting, food, turkeys, and multicultural books for attendees. We were creating the web, and taking action, using the network we had built.

The web continued to grow beyond the annual "Thanks 4 Giving" event, developing into other opportunities to give back to the community in meaningful ways. I travel to the Ramsey County Juvenile Detention Center once or twice a month to mentor and give haircuts to incarcerated youth. This has recently expanded to an opportunity to do the Ramsey County Adult Detention Center, with potential for healing circles and book clubs in both facilities. The impact we can make is limitless.

An unexpected aspect of my journey that I had never imagined is becoming a teacher in various capacities. Through Sola Salons, I offer classes for upcoming barbers and hair stylists to learn how to fading and blending techniques. These public classes are held several times a year. Surprisingly, I was offered a teaching role at the Cosmetology program at Saint Paul College, where I was once told that I'd never succeed as a barber. For the past few years, I've taught cosmetology students my licensed techniques. Talk about things coming full circle!

Sharing my experiences with others can lead to unforeseen outcomes. Looking back at my journey, there were always people who shared wisdom, guided me, supported me, and gave me opportunities. They never gave up on me, and allowed me to shine despite my imperfections. They saw potential in me that I didn't always myself. I truly believe everything happened for a reason, and there are lessons in every experience. It all depends on our perspective.

I created the web that now includes my family, friends, the community, clients, business relationships, and countless others I've met along the way. It's an acknowledgement that we are all connected in ways beyond our understanding.

At the center of the web is the Nabors family; my mom, dad, my wife Amy, my children and my siblings. This is where it all began, and through them, and by the grace of God, I learned how to create the web.

CONCLUSION

According to research by the US Department of Health & Human Services in 2015, over 100,000 people are waiting for lifesaving kidney transplants in the United States. The average wait time for an individual needing their first kidney transplant is over 3.5 years. In 2014, out of 17,107 transplants, 11,570 came from deceased donors, while 5,537 were from living donors. On average, more than 3,000 new patients are added to the kidney transplant waiting list each month.

Tragically, 13 people die each day while waiting for a kidney transplant, and every 14 minutes a person is added to the waiting list. Research indicates that in 2014, over 4,700 patients died while waiting for a transplant, and more than 3,600 people became too ill to receive one. Chronic kidney disease affects over 1 in 7 adults, impacting more than 37 million people in the U.S., with as many as 9 in 10 unaware they have the disease. This condition is more prevalent among Black Americans, who face longer waiting periods; the average wait time for Black patients is 59.9 months (4.9 years) compared to 41.3 months (3.4 years) for White patients. As of August 2021, over 90,000 people were on the waiting list to for a kidney transplant, the majority of whom were on dialysis. According to the CDC, every 24 hours, 360 people begin dialysis treatment for kidney failure.

Every day, as I drive to Nabors Cut, I pass by the very place where I received my dialysis treatments. Instead of feeling ashamed of my past, I take pride in what I've overcome. I want to inspire those who feel like the odds are stacked against them. Who did I have to look up to during my time on dialysis? Who could I admire that had received a transplant and was thriving?

Dialysis was debilitating; it left me physically depleted, damaged my eyesight, and significantly impacted my mental and spiritual health. Many people close to me have been on dialysis or received kidney transplants—some did not survive, while others are now living vibrant lives. Not everyone has been as fortunate as I have been. I consider myself blessed. To God be the glory.

Asé.

In retrospect, I often sit back and ask myself, "What iF?"

WHAT IF? (POEM)

?What iF I never needed a Kidney Transplant.

?What iF my wife wasn't 5 months pregnant with our 1st child and we hadn't just recently agreed for her to be a stay at home mom.

?What iF the Nephrologist didn't say to me "You have to start Dialysis before it's to late" with a Creatinine of 19.5

?What iF I didn't have to rush straight to Dialysis the same day after the birth of my son.

?What iF I didn't Dialyze for 11 months 3X's a week for 3 1/2 hrs. and lose 10 pounds every session.
?What iF my brother Reggie never gave me one of his Kidneys.

?What iF that month of Plasmapheresis didn't work when the Doctors thought my brothers Kidney was rejecting.

?What if I had never gotten sick and my Primary Doctor & Nephrologist didn't agree to prescribe me Augmentin that caused me to Vomit & Diarrhea for 3 straight weeks which dehydrated me and I lost my brothers Kidney of 9 years.

?What iF I didn't have to go back on Dialysis for 14 more months.

?What iF they didn't cut me open so far to place the Catheter in my chest I would not of lost so much blood and needed blood transfusions.

?What iF in the hospital the elevator would have opened up when transportation was taking me in a wheelchair to my eye appointment when my vision was severely damaged and I was on the phone with my wife telling her my every move when I passed out with her on the phone not knowing transportation was yelling my name calling for help with her still on the line.

?What iF that old man waiting on his wife at Dialysis didn't stop me to talk as I'm walking out the door thinking I needed exercise after getting off the machine so I was going to take the stairs but ended up passing out at the door .

?What iF my family would have left me.

?What iF the City didn't want to take our house when we asked to make payment arrangements after never being late the 11 years we lived there.

?What iF my wife didn't get our house back and hold everything down while raising our 3 kids.

?What iF we didn't get 3 benefits thrown for us and countless
support from family, friends and strangers.

?What iF my Dad never gave me one of his Kidneys.

?What iF the 2 Hospital employees would of listened to me right before surgery when I asked to see a doctor because I was having an allergic reaction to the Pre-Med.

?What iF the surgeon didn't tell my wife they had to reverse all the pain meds during surgery because I was having an allergic reaction so when I came to I was in excruciating pain for hours and couldn't see.

?What iF the doctors would of listened to me and my wife when we told them for 3 straight days that me being in pain not being able to move my right leg isn't normal come to find out I had a blood clot sitting on my nerve so they had to reopen the Kidney Transplant.

?What iF I would of entertained the suicidal thoughts.

?What iF I didn't survive Covid

?What iF I didn't have to take 20-27 pills a day for the rest of my life.

?What iF I didn't have to get a needle in my arm once a month for the rest of my life.

?What iF my parents wouldn't have raised me to NEVER GIVE UP

?What iF GOD has a plan for me.

?What iF this happened to you

The thing about ?What IF is that we'll never know...

Happy 10 year Kidney Anniversary To Me For Never Giving Up

~ ROBERT NABORS

PHOTO GALLERY

Robert at his shop preparing for next
appointment (2022)

Bobby (Dad), Reggie, and Robert Nabors following interview

Reggie Nabors following interview (2020)

Robert and his Dad following interview (2020)

Robert and Reggie following interview (2020)

Bobby Nabors (Dad) following interview (2020)

Behind the scenes of interview (2020)

Saba (Sean Stewart) following interview (2020)

Saba (Sean Stewart) following interview (2020)

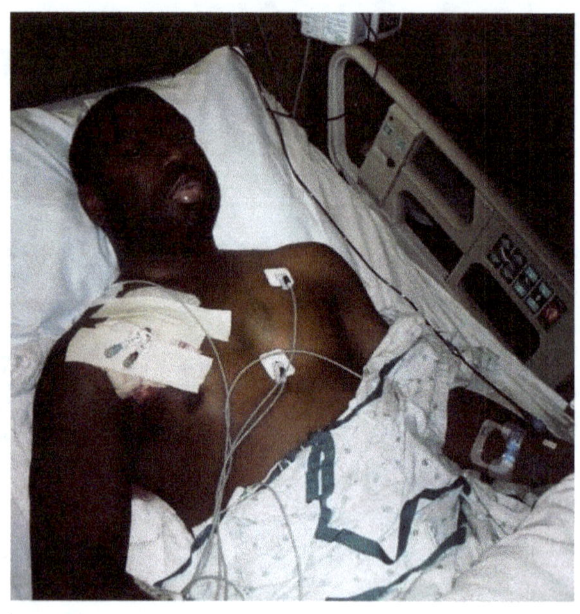

Robert after being hospitalized prior to 2nd transplant (2010)

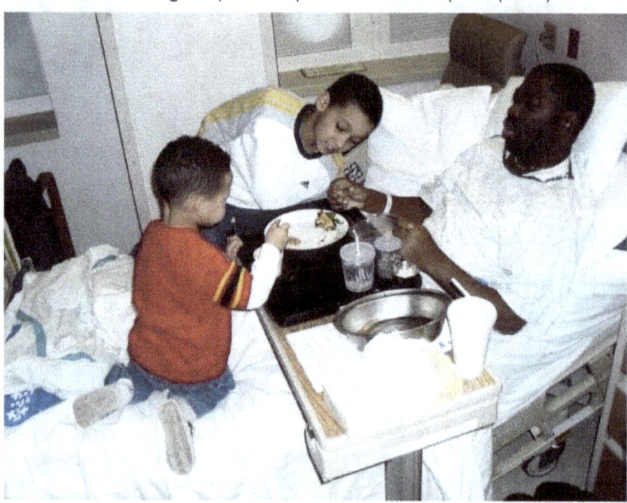

Blood transfusion after going back on dialysis (2010)

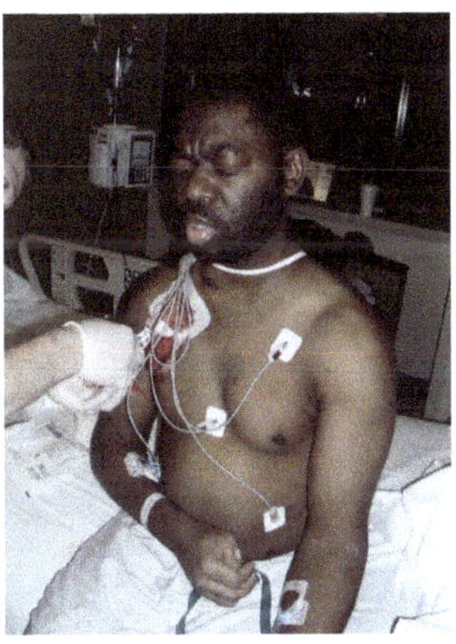

Robert going back on dialysis
(2010)

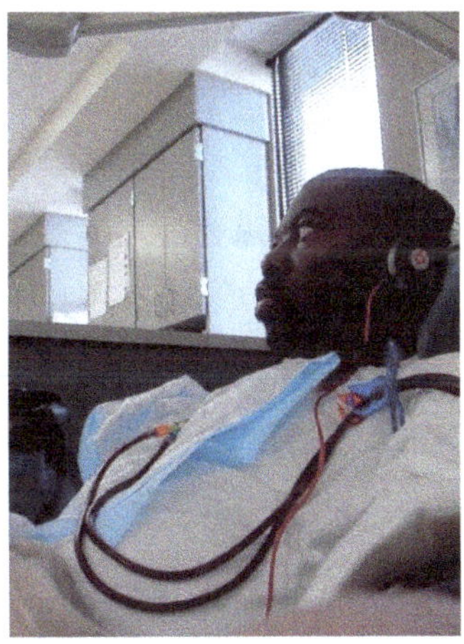

Robert on dialysis machine
(2010)

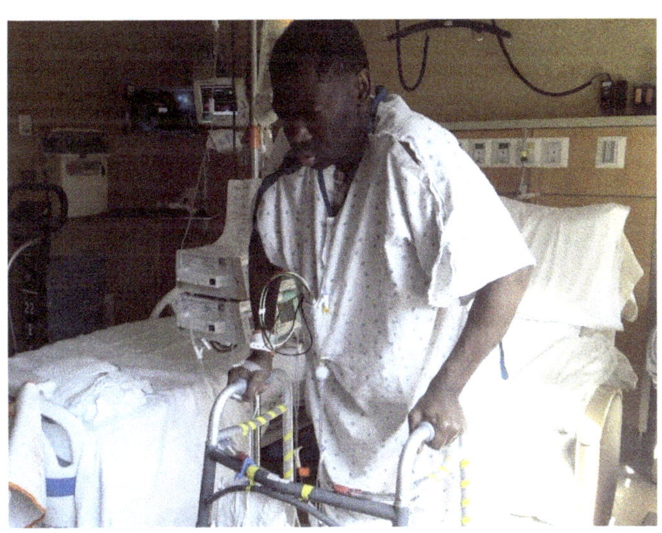

Robert in hospital, using walker after 2nd transplant (2012)

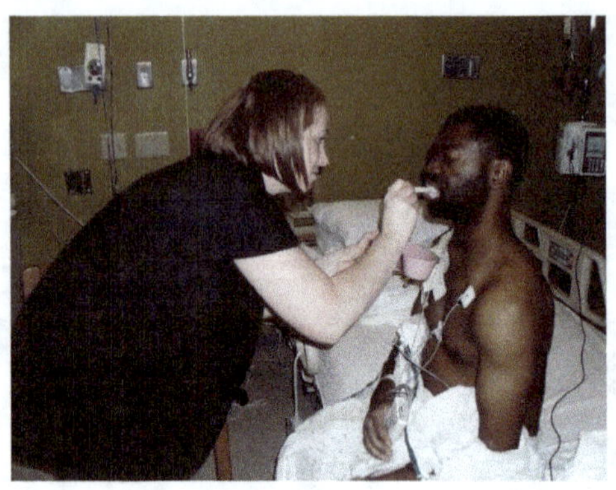

Amy brushing Robert's teeth in hospital (above
2010)

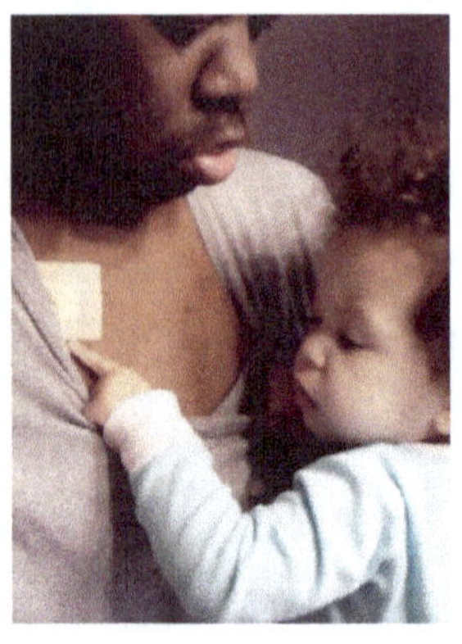

Robert on dialysis machine (2010)

Robert and Amber pointing
at bandage (2010)

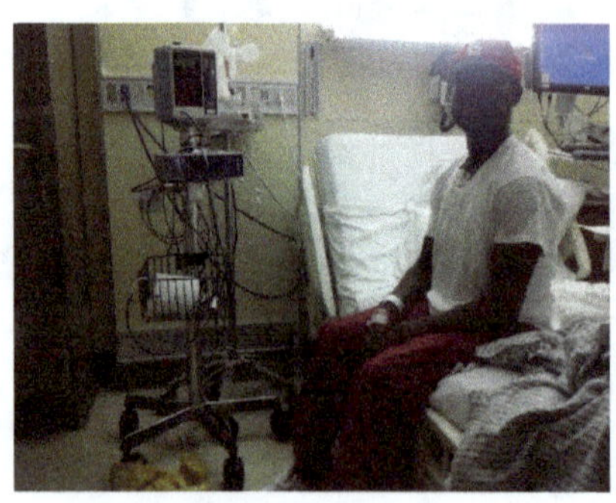

Robert following kidney transplant (2012)

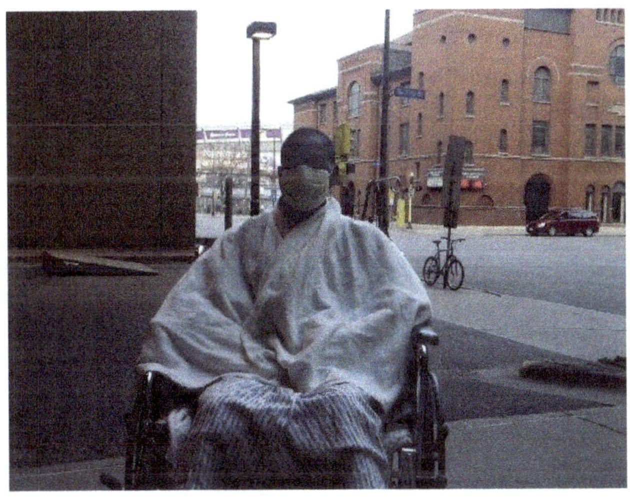

Robert following second Kidney Transplant (2012)

Robert 9 years following kidney transplant (2021)

THREE BENEFITS

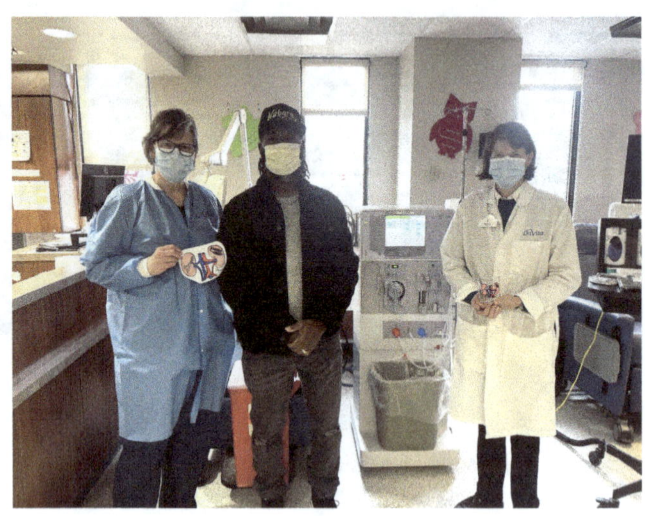

DOCTORS, NURSES & DIALYSIS TECHNICIANS

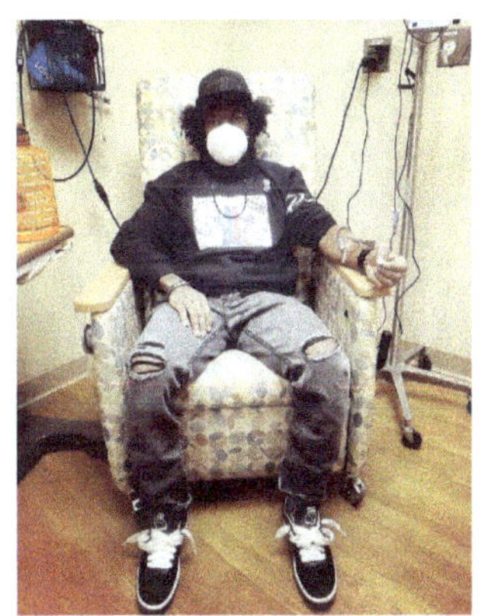 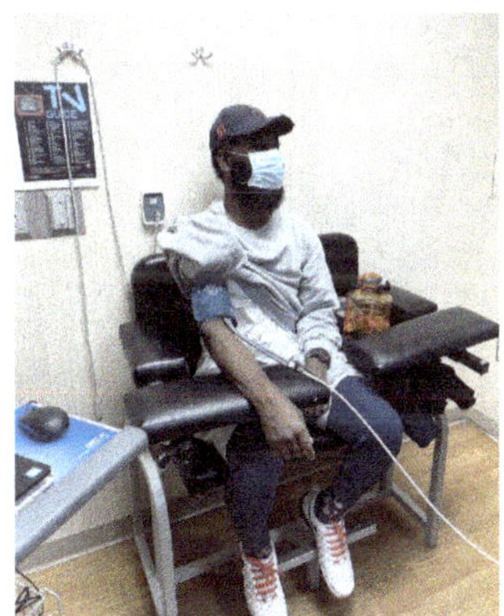

MONTHLY LABS & DAILY MEDICATION

AMY & ROBERT NABORS

FAMILY TIES

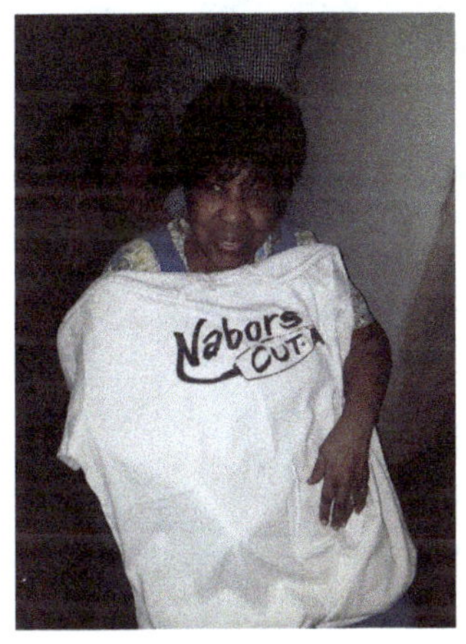

Robert and Angie (top left/right). Robert, Angie, Reggie and Ronnie (bottom)

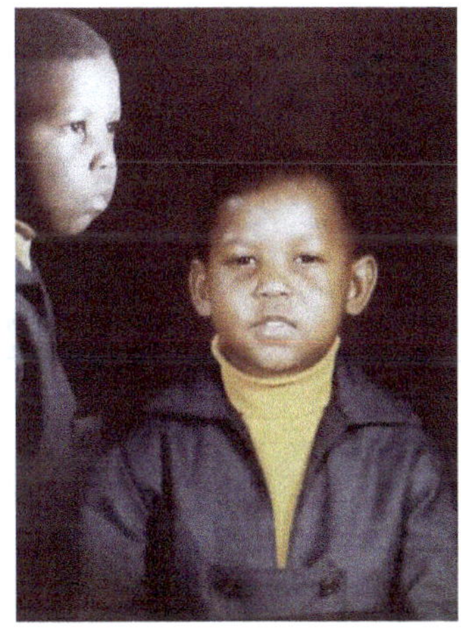

Robert at 6 years old (1981)

Robert, Angie and Reggie (1980)

Robert, Angie with their Mom and Dad (1977)

Robert, Angie, Reggie, Ronnie and Kenyanna (1985)

Robert, Angie, Reggie, Aketo, Cassius, Tom, Teremy, Tony, Glover (Ashland Avenue)

Young Robert and Angie

Angie

Robert, Reggie and Ronnie
(2014)

Robert and Ronnie

Mom (Ceretta)

Robert and his Mom

HIGHLAND PARK

BACKSTAGE BARBER DAYS

FAMILY & FRIENDS

NABORS CUT

ANNUAL THANKS 4 GIVING EVENT

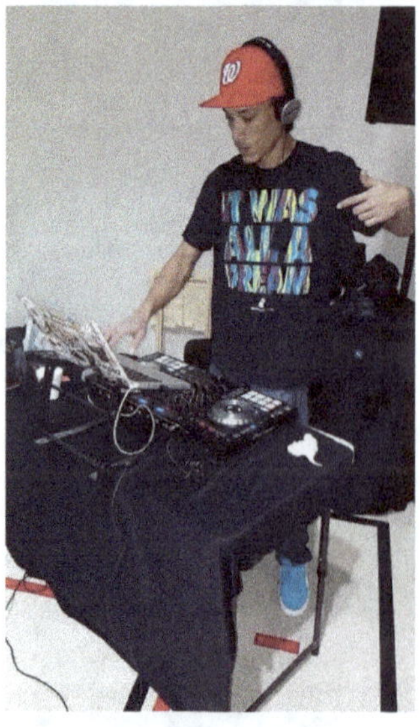

RAMSEY COUNTY A.D.C. & J.D.C.

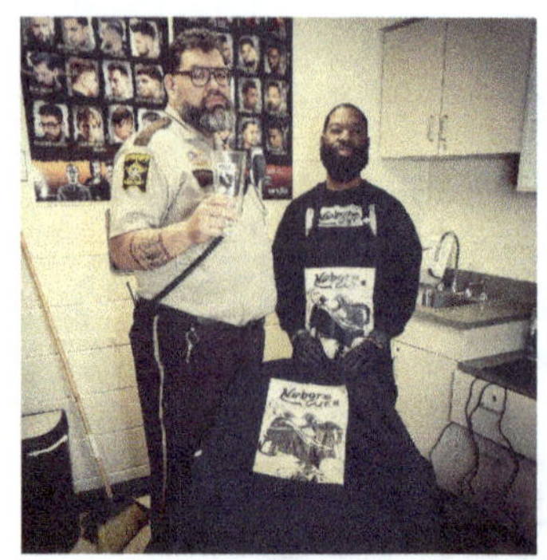

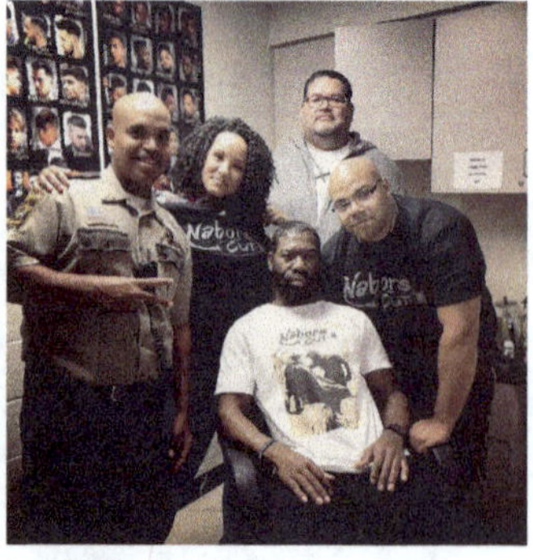

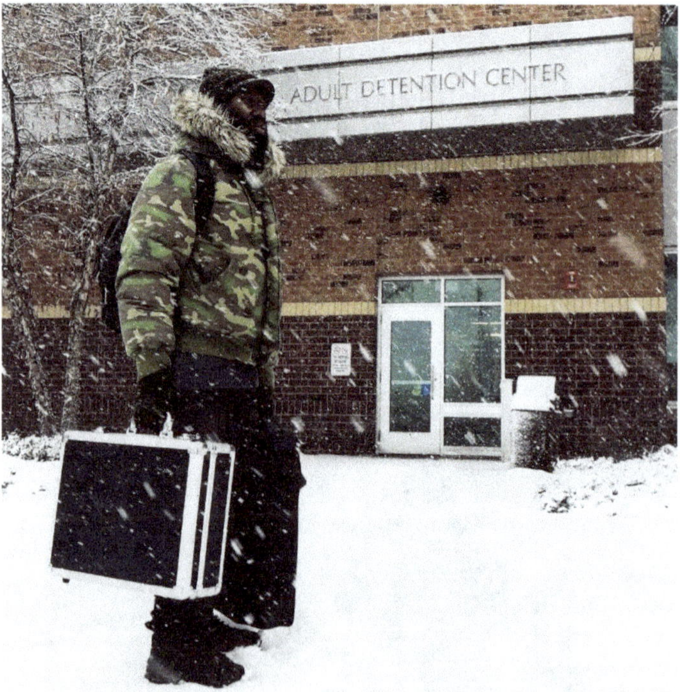
ADULT DETENTION CENTER

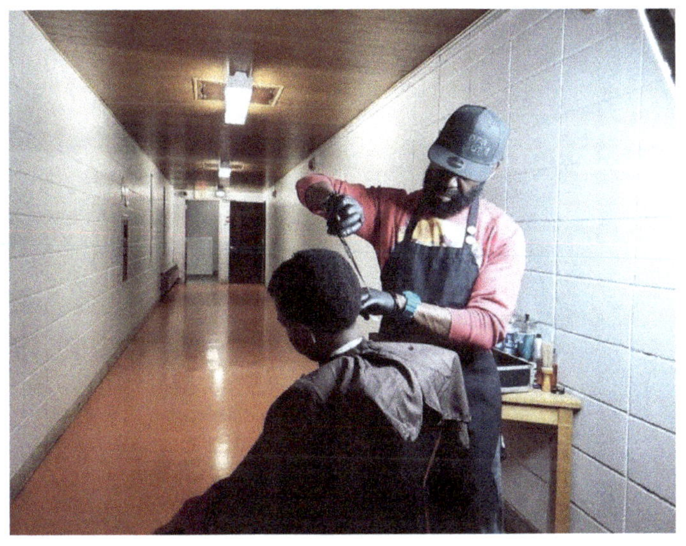

BOYS TOTEM TOWN

Nabors
CUT 1

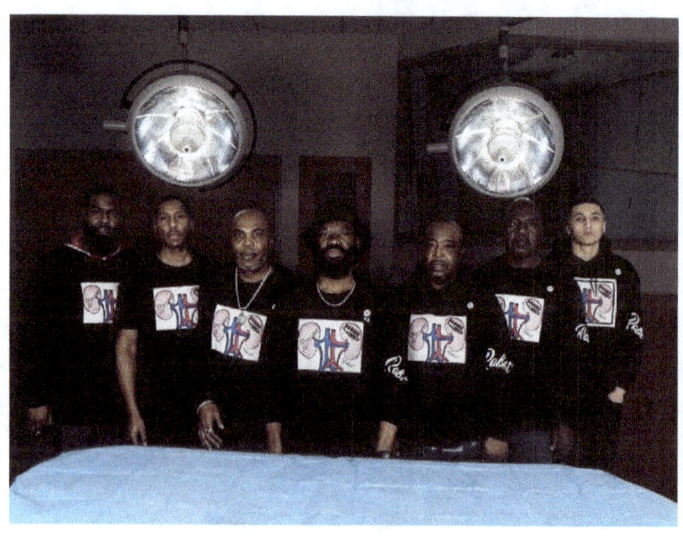

BIBLIOGRAPHY & REFERENCES

Center of Disease Control and Prevention (2022, December 28) DC Testing: Everything You Need To Know. Retrieved from https://www.cdc.gov/kidneydisease/publications-resources/kidney-tests.html#:~:text=Serum%20creatinine.&text=Normal%20levels%20for%20you%20will,not%20working%20like%20they%20should.

Center of Disease Control and Prevention (2022, February 13) Your Risk of C. diff (Clostridioides difficile). Retrieved from https://www.cdc.gov/cdiff/risk.html

Eric B and Rakim (1992). *Don't Sweat The Technique* https://en.m.wikipedia.org/wiki/Don%27t_Sweat_the_Technique

Eric B and Rakim (1987). *Paid in Full* https://en.m.wikipedia.org/wiki/Paid_in_Full_(album)

Esposito, Lisa (2022 April 1) When to Worry About Creatinine Levels. Retrieved from https://health.usnews.com/health-care/patient-advice/articles/creatininelevels

Frederick Douglas Quote
https://www.brainyquote.com/quotes/frederick_douglass_201574

Jay Z (1998). Lyrics from the song "A week Ago"
https://en.m.wikipedia.org/wiki/Vol._2..._Hard_Knock-_Life

Beyoncé (2008). Lyrics from the song "Single Ladies"
https://en.m.wikipedia.org/wiki/
Single_Ladies_(Put_a_Ring_on_It)

Mayo Clinic (2022, December 20) C . difficile Infection. Retrieved from https://www.mayoclinic.org/diseases-conditions/c-difficile/symptoms-causes/
syc-20351691

MC Hammer (1988). Lyrics from the song "Turn that mother out" https://en.m.wikipedia.org/wiki/
Let%27s_Get_It_Started_(album)

Michael Jackson, Thriller (1982)
https://en.m.wikipedia.org/wiki/Thriller_(album)

National Institute of Diabetes and Digestive and Kidney Diseases (2023 March 12) Kidney Disease Statistics for the United States. Retrieved from
https://www.niddk.nih.gov/health-information/health-statistics/kidney-disease

National Kidney Foundation (2023, March 8) Kidney Basics. Retrieved from https://www.kidney.org/kidney-basics

National Kidney Foundation (2023, March 10) Plasmapheresis and Blood type Incompatible Kidney Transplant. Retrieved from https://www.kidney.org/atoz/content/plasmapheresis#:~:text=Plasmapheresis%20before%20transplant%20removes%20antibodies,may%20also%20be%20administered%20intravenously.

National Kidney Foundation (2023, March 7) What To Expect After Donation. Retrieved from https://www.kidney.org/transplantation/livingdonors/what-expect-after-donation

National Organ Foundation (2023 March 8) Organ Donation and Transplant Statistics. Retrieved from https://www.kidney.org/news/newsroom/factsheets/Organ-Donation-and-Transplantation-Stats

NYC Point Gods (2021). Showtime https://deadline.com/2022/06/nyc-point-gods-documentary-kenny-anderson-mark-jackson-stephon-marbury-showtime-airdate-nba-1235037077/amp/

Prince (1984). *Purple Rain* https://en.m.wikipedia.org/wiki/Purple_Rain_(album)

Merriam Webster (2019). Merriam-Webster. Retrieved from https://www.merriam-webster.com/dictionary/protégé

Ralls, Eric (2022, December 31) Lotus Flower How Does a Lotus Flower Grow: The Life Cycle of a Lotus. Retrieved from https://www.earth.com/earthpedia-articles/how-does-a-lotus-flower-grow/

The Breakdown (1955) by Alfred Hitchcock https://www.complete-hitchcock.com/Breakdown.html

Thrilla in Manila (1975) https://en.m.wikipedia.org/wiki/Thrilla_in_Manila

Wichita Nephrology Group (2022 December 29) When Do Patients require dialysis? Retrieved from https://wichitanephrology.com/case-study/patients-require-dialysis/#:~:text=Usually%2C%20when%20the%20creatinine%20clearance,about%20the%20need%20for%20dialysis.